THE
JACOBY
& MEYERS

PRACTICAL GUIDE TO

PERSONAL INJURY

Gail J. Koff
FOUNDING PARTNER,
JACOBY & MEYERS LAW OFFICES

SIMON & SCHUSTER
New York   London   Toronto
Sydney   Tokyo   Singapore

SIMON & SCHUSTER
Simon & Schuster Building
Rockefeller Center
1230 Avenue of the Americas
New York, New York, 10020

Designed by Irving Perkins Associates
Manufactured in the United States of America

1 3 5 7 9 10 8 6 4 2

Library of Congress Cataloging-in-Publication Data
Koff, Gail J.
The Jacoby & Meyers practical guide to personal injury : Gail J. Koff.
p. cm.
Includes index.
1. Personal injuries—United States—Popular works. I. Jacoby &
Meyers (Firm) II. Title. III. Title: Jacoby and Meyers practical
guide to personal injury. IV. Title: Practical guide to personal injury.
KF1257.Z9K64   1991
346.7303′23—dc20
[347.306323]   91-26830
CIP

ISBN: 0-671-72683-8

For my mother, Sylvia J. Koff,
who was the victim of an automobile accident

The purpose of this book is to educate you about legal matters so that you can deal more effectively with your lawyer. Federal and state laws are constantly changing. Consult your attorney about how the laws apply to your current case.

CONTENTS

PART TWO
HOW TO HELP YOURSELF:
CASE STUDIES IN PERSONAL INJURY

INTRODUCTION

NEARLY TWENTY YEARS ago, we established the law firm of Jacoby & Meyers with the primary intention of filling a "legal niche" that we believed had, up until then, been virtually ignored. That niche consisted of the millions of middle-income Americans who had been denied, primarily due to high costs and the mystique surrounding the legal profession, easy access to quality legal representation.

For two decades now, our firm has been the leader in the movement to make quality legal representation available to everyone, regardless of social or economic status. This book is part of our continuing effort to demystify the legal process and promote cooperation and understanding between attorney and client. The book explores in particular the subject of personal injury.

Accidents that result in personal injury are surprisingly common. Unfortunately, most people tend to be uninformed about the significant cost and emotional pain that such accidents can cause. People also tend to be uninformed about their legal rights and the recoveries available to them in the event of personal injury. Thus the primary purpose of this book is to help people through the trauma of an accident by explaining how personal injury law and the legal system pertaining to it work. We discuss the various kinds of accidents, and also such subjects as choosing the proper attorney and suing the government. Along the way, we try to shed light on the negligence and medical malpractice controversy, as well as on the sometimes confusing and always complex subject of automobile insurance.

A few words about the organization of the book. The first half contains background material on topics such as the definition of a personal injury case; how to value your case; whether or not you actually have a viable case; how to choose the right attorney; and how the legal system in personal injury cases works—from negotiation and settlement straight through to litigation. In the second half of the book, we focus on specific kinds of accidents—accidents to children, premises liability, product liability, motor vehicle accidents, and medical malpractice—by presenting real cases, which, we hope, will give the reader a good idea of how the law works in specific instances. The situations presented are all based on actual cases handled by our firm. However, in order to protect the privacy of our clients, we have altered the facts and changed names and locations.

Efforts have also been made to give appropriate evaluations for the verdicts and settlements of these cases. But again, for reasons of confidentiality, we have altered the figures somewhat. Further, it is important to understand the impossibility of transferring the settlement or verdict figures from one case to another. Every case is different and, even if the difference is slight, the changes in the factual pattern will inevitably affect the recovery obtained. Also, it is inevitable that different juries will come back with different verdicts. For instance, in New York State, the Bronx is known as a liberal jurisdiction, hence verdicts may be larger; whereas Westchester County is conservative and thus verdicts are likely to be smaller. For these reasons, there can be no across-the-board prediction of what settlements or verdicts can or will be. As tempting as it might seem, you cannot compare a potential recovery in your case with someone else's case. After all, attorneys may argue the case, but the facts determine its outcome.

Another caveat. Because laws and procedures vary from state to state, we have tried to present the general principles of law and explain how these principles are applied in *most* but certainly not all instances. Therefore, you should not rely solely on this book for information on specific laws regarding your case. Your attorney will know what laws and procedures apply to your case in your jurisdiction. It is certainly possible to handle many legal situations without hiring an attorney. However, due to the complexity of personal injury law, if you are the victim of an accident, you should, in almost all cases, consult an attorney. We strongly believe that the better prepared and more responsive you are as a client, the better the job your attorney can do for you. Your cooperation and understanding will certainly have a favorable impact on any recovery you may receive.

As careful as we all might try be, accidents are, unfortunately, a part of life. We hope that if you are the victim of an accident, this book will help you through the aftermath. If, as we hope, you never have to use it, you may want to read and keep it simply as a reference.

PART ONE

WHAT TO DO,

WHERE TO GO, AND

WHAT YOU MUST KNOW

CHAPTER ONE

PERSONAL INJURY:

AN OVERVIEW

A WOMAN PURCHASES a can of aerosol hairspray from her local drugstore. The next morning, she opens the can in her bathroom, which happens to be directly adjacent to her kitchen, and prepares to use it. Unfortunately, the valve is faulty and after she releases the button the spray continues to flow. When she inadvertently points it in the direction of the kitchen, the hairspray is ignited by the pilot light on the stove. As a result, her face is badly burned.

Can she sue for her injuries? Whom does she sue? What kind of compensation is she entitled to? Must she sue within a certain period of time to preserve her rights?

A two-year-old child runs into the bathroom and locks himself in. He climbs into the bathtub and turns on the hot water tap. The water temperature is close to 200 degrees, well above the safe limit, and his feet are severely scalded.

Do the child and his mother have an action to recover for the damages to the boy? And if so, whom do they have an action against?

. . .

You invite a friend over to visit. It snowed the night before her visit and you have neglected to remove the snow and ice from the steps in front of your house. Your friend slips on the ice and breaks her leg.

Are you responsible for the injuries suffered by your friend? Does your insurance cover your liability?

In this country literally millions of accidental injuries occur each year. The majority are the result of automobile accidents or simple slips and falls. But there are others that may be due to defective products, unsafe premises, or the carelessness or incompetence of a doctor, dentist, or mechanic. Many are serious enough to require medical attention.

But whatever the injury, if it was caused by someone else's intentional or negligent behavior, whether through an action that shouldn't have been taken or the failure to do something that should have been done, you may have the basis for a lawsuit. If that lawsuit is successful, you may be compensated not only for your medical expenses, but also for the money you lose because of time missed from work, the cost of any rehabilitation to your body and mind, and tuition fees for retraining you for a new occupation if you are no longer able to perform your former job. In some cases you might even be compensated for the psychological harm and pain you suffered.

Today, one of the most common types of litigation handled by our court system has to do with personal injury. More than seven hundred thousand accident cases were filed in federal and state courts in 1985. Today, the number has probably risen to well over a million, and this does not include the millions of other cases that are settled by attorneys before they are ever filed in court. Nor does it take into account those cases, perhaps also numbering in the millions, that are never pursued because the victims are ignorant of their rights under the law.

Other statistics concerning accidents are no less astounding. For instance:

- According to a recent study, accidental injuries kill more Americans between the ages of one and thirty-four than all diseases put together. These fatal accidents drain the economy of more years of working life than cancer and heart disease combined.
- Among the ten leading causes of death for our total population, accidents (other than car accidents) rank fourth. Car accidents rank sixth, and they alone account for fifty thousand deaths and five hundred thousand injuries each year.
- For every fatal accident there are approximately ten nonfatal accidental injuries.
- According to the U.S. Consumer Product Safety Commission, for each of the last three years an average of ninety-thousand children under the age of fifteen received hospital emergency room treatment as a result of injuries from toys.
- In 1988, thirty-five deaths and more than eighteen thousand injuries requiring hospital treatment occurred as the result of power lawnmower accidents, while each year an estimated 350 children under the age of five drown in residential swimming pools and spas, and each year approximately 4,600 children under the age of five are treated in hospital emergency rooms following water submersion accidents.
- One out of twenty-five Americans this year is likely to be an accident victim.

With these facts in mind, it should come as no surprise that you or some member of your family may one day become the victim of an accident that results in personal injury. If so, there are a number of questions you should ask yourself and a number of factors you must consider before consulting a personal injury attorney.

DO YOU HAVE A CASE?

When either your property or your person is damaged you have certain basic rights, which are determined by the law of torts (the word *tort* is derived from the French word meaning *wrong*). For example, when a person acting in a negligent fashion injures you or damages your property, that person is responsible for paying for the damage he caused.

In this country the only compensation for a tort is money, and the amount is determined, if the case comes to trial, in the civil rather than the criminal courts. The civil courts are a means of awarding fair compensation for, among other things, the results of accidents that are caused by someone else's negligence. However, it is a common misconception that simply because you have been injured in an accident, you are automatically entitled to some kind of compensation. Unfortunately, that is not the case.

Essentially, there are three criteria which must be met in order for a valid personal injury case to exist. First, the person who caused the accident had to have some type of duty of reasonable care to the person who was injured. For instance, anyone driving a car must conform to certain reasonable standards of care, such as driving within the posted speed limits, obeying traffic signals, and keeping the automobile in good working condition. Another example is the storeowner who has a duty to maintain his property in a safe manner (promptly cleaning up spills, for instance). This standard applies to homeowners and landlords as well.

The second element of a personal injury case is that there must be a breach of that duty of reasonable care. In the case of an automobile accident, for example, that breach would occur if someone was driving carelessly or ignoring speed limits and stop signs. With a storeowner, failure to take reasonable steps to make the business premises safe for the public by keeping floors free of debris and spills would be such a breach.

Homeowners and landlords who allow unsafe conditions on their property also breach the duty of reasonable care.

The third element of any negligence case concerns the proximate or legal cause of the accident. This means that the breach of duty of reasonable care, or the negligent act, must have actually caused the accident and the injury. For example, suppose there is a broken step on a stairway in an office building, and the owner is or should have been aware of it. In legal terms, this is called notice and it is an important element of liability. The person responsible should have known about the dangerous situation and had reasonable time to rectify it. The owner of the office building in our example has a duty to repair that broken step within a reasonable time or take other measures to eliminate the risk of injury, such as warning people about it. If the step is not repaired and if you are not warned about it and, as a result, you fall and are injured, you have a case. However, if you fall on the stairs due to clumsiness and not as a result of tripping on the faulty step, you do not have a case.

In other words, a person is not responsible for paying damages unless he is legally considered to be at fault for an accident. In some accidents, there is no legal fault. They just happen, even though everyone involved may have been paying attention and have fulfilled any duty of reasonable care. For instance, suppose that a tree limb breaks as the result of being struck by lightning. It falls and hits your car while you are in it, causing property damage and personal injury. This would qualify as an "act of God," and no one would be at fault. In cases like these, the victim would usually be responsible for paying for any damage to his or her person or property.

DAMAGE

Even when there is legal liability on the part of the person who caused the accident, the victim still must also be able to prove that there have been injuries and damage caused by the accident. If there is no damage, then no matter how serious the breach of duty of reasonable care might have been, there is no basis for legal action. To use a common sports term, no harm, no foul.

For instance, suppose that you go to a doctor and obtain a prescription. You then go to your local pharmacist and, due to a mix-up, you are given the wrong drug. However, when you get home you realize the mistake and don't take the drug. There is certainly negligence on the part of your pharmacist, but since you did not take the drug and were not harmed, there is no damage. Hence, there is no case.

Another common example is discovering a foreign object in food. If you found a piece of glass in a newly opened jar of peaches, unless you actually swallowed it and it did some kind of damage to your person, you don't have a case. In both these instances, there is liability; that is, there was a duty of reasonable care and that duty was breached. But there is no injury and consequently no case.

If there is damage, however, it must be serious enough to warrant an action. For instance, suppose that you walk into a store and, in front of the fruit and vegetable section, you slip and fall on several grapes, which, through the testimony of eyewitnesses, you can prove have been on the floor for well over an hour, certainly long enough for the storeowner to have found them and cleaned them up. However, your injury is minor: a bruised knee that requires no medical attention and does not cause you to miss any work. There is liability: The storeowner had the responsibility to police the floors and clean up any debris. In his failure to do this he violated his duty of reasonable care to you. There was even an injury: your bruised knee. But the damage was so slight that legal action would not be justified. The expense for that action would be more than any compensation you would receive for such an injury.

ACTIONABLE (TORTIOUS) CONDUCT

In deciding whether you have a personal injury case, you must consider the question of actionable conduct. If the conduct that caused your injury was criminal, your only redress may be through the criminal court system. The criminal, if found guilty, is punished, but you receive no compensation for your injury or any damage to your property. If, however, the conduct that caused your injury was tortious, you may seek redress by filing suit in civil court. Sometimes conduct is both criminal and tortious, resulting in a civil suit as well as a criminal prosecution based on the same actionable conduct. For instance, if a drunk driver causes a collision, that drunk driver may be arrested and tried for a criminal offense as well as being sued in civil court for compensation for the injuries and damage caused by the accident.

There are three kinds of tortious conduct that may result in civil action: negligence, intentional misconduct, and some acts that give rise to what is known as strict liability.

Negligence

Negligence is the most common type of actionable conduct or tort and, generally speaking, it may be most simply defined as carelessness. A fall on a wet floor, being hit by an automobile that went through a stop sign, and tripping over a broken step are all examples of accidents caused by someone's negligence. In such cases you have the right to seek compensation for your injury.

Intentional Misconduct

Although we are primarily concerned with accidents, it is important to know and understand what constitutes intentional misconduct, or an intentional tort. If someone deliberately tries to hurt you or damage your property, it is an intentional tort. The difference between negligence and an intentional tort is the state of mind of the person who is responsible. Negligence is carelessness, while an intentional tort is an act done deliberately.

Among the various categories of intentional torts in most

jurisdictions are assault (an act that reasonably causes you to be in fear of being hit), battery (a deliberate and offensive touching of any kind without permission), false imprisonment, theft, defamation, intentional damage or destruction of personal property, and fraud.

If you are the victim of an intentional tort, you may be entitled to recover what is referred to as punitive damages in addition to any compensatory damages you are awarded. Along with compensatory damages, the amount of punitive damages is also left up to a jury to decide, and the purpose of such damages is to punish the wrongdoer and deter others from similar misbehavior.

The jury's discretion in the matter of punitive damages has long been a thorn in the side of defendants in intentional tort cases, who argue that there should be a limit on the amount of punitive damages a jury can award. In fact, there is a case now in front of the Supreme Court that will probably decide the matter. The case concerns Cleopatra Haslip, who was sold an insurance policy that, as it turned out, did not cover her treatment for a kidney infection, leaving her with no coverage for $3,500 of medical bills. In a lawsuit filed against the insurer, Mrs. Haslip and three coworkers claimed they were defrauded by an agent of the Pacific Mutual Life Insurance Company. A Birmingham, Alabama, jury returned a verdict for the plaintiffs in the amount of $1,077,978, most of which was assessed as punitive damages.

This case concerns the issue of whether, under the "due process" clause of the Fourteenth Amendment, juries must be given limiting standards to guide their decisions on when punitive damages should be assessed and how much they can award. The defendants, along with other big businesses that have filed briefs in the case, argue that punitive damage verdicts are completely out of hand, and that the risk of potential punitive damage verdicts frightens companies so much that they are unwilling to introduce new products to the marketplace. On the other hand, as Consumers Union of United States spokeswoman Linda Lipsen argues, "Punitive damages are a very effective tool to curb outrageous misconduct by companies."

In March 1991, the Supreme Court affirmed the decision specifically upholding the punitive damages award.

Strict Liability

Any situation that holds uncommon danger and great likelihood of harm may come under the heading of ultrahazardous activities (for example, blasting operations, nuclear power and chemical plants, keeping wild animals on your property, or crop dusting), for which there is strict liability. In cases that fall under the heading of ultrahazardous activities, you are usually permitted to recover damages for injury caused by the activity without having to prove that the defendant did anything wrong, because the defendant is under strict liability.

For instance, suppose that there is a construction project taking place next door to your home, which includes some blasting. As the result of one of these explosions, serious structural damage is caused to your house. You would be entitled to recover damages regardless of whether there was actual negligence on the part of those doing the blasting. The reasoning behind this is that the activity is so inherently dangerous that strict liability is automatically imposed. Even the fact that the defendant took all reasonable precautions does not constitute a defense in cases like these.

Another area of strict liability law involves defective products. When any product has a defective design, or a manufacturing flaw, or is dangerous without giving buyers adequate warnings or instructions, the law makes manufacturers and sellers strictly liable for harm caused by the defective product. Because it is so difficult for an injured consumer to prove exactly what negligence on the part of the manufacturer led to the defect in the product, fairness has led the courts to adopt this doctrine and relieve the injured party of the burden of showing negligence. (This very technical and complex area of personal injury law is discussed more thoroughly in Chapter 9.)

WHAT CONSTITUTES NEGLIGENCE?

Once an accident has occurred and significant damage has been caused, you must ascertain whether the person who caused the accident was negligent. The legal standard that is applied is whether, under the circumstances, that person was exercising "due care." Of course, due care is a rather vague term and in defining it a number of factors—such as the circumstances of the accident and the age and physical and mental condition of the parties involved—must be taken into consideration.

Generally speaking, conduct is measured against what a reasonable adult person of similar physical and mental condition would or should have done in the same situation. Children and the elderly are held to a somewhat different standard of due care. In the case of a child the standard is what a reasonable child of the same age, experience, and intelligence would or should have done. Obviously, you can't expect a three-year-old to behave in the same way as an eleven-year-old. In fact, in many states children under the age of seven are not capable of being legally negligent. Thus, even if a child under this age does cause an accident, you may not sue the child, although you may be able to sue the parent for lack of supervision. However, if a child is performing an activity that only an adult is allowed to perform (such as driving a car), the standard changes and the child is then measured by what would be expected of an adult.

By the same token, a person with a physical disability that affected his actions in a given case would not be held to the same standard of due care as one without that physical disability. For example, someone suffering a hearing loss would not be held to as high a standard as someone with normal hearing in a case in which the person's hearing loss affected his ability to act. Similarly, the elderly might also not be held to the same standard of due care.

Generally, anyone guilty of a tort is financially responsible for the damage that flows directly from his or her act. There are, however, some exceptions. Public officials or peace officers while in the performance of their duty may not be liable for their actions if it is decided that they were necessary for either the public safety or general welfare.

Federal and state governments may not be sued unless they authorize it. This principle stems from the common law rule under which subjects were forbidden to sue their king. Later, this rule was amended to allow suits against the king, but only with his permission. In this country, you may sue the government but only under certain circumstances and within certain guidelines. (These, along with the rules governing lawsuits against government agencies and municipalities, will be discussed in Chapter 12).

Employers are held liable for all acts of employees that are performed within the scope of their employment. This would include any torts that might be committed while on the job. Corporations are also held liable for the tortious actions of their employees.

Normally, a spouse is not responsible for the torts of the other spouse as long as he or she did not instigate, coerce, or endorse the acts of that spouse. However, in community property states, an award for damages against one spouse can be sought and obtained from the assets they hold in common.

Pet owners are, under most circumstances and in many jurisdictions, not held liable for the "first bite," unless they are aware that their pet is dangerous. In that case, they are responsible for maintaining control over their animal, and they are negligent and liable for damages if they do not and an accident occurs.

PROVING NEGLIGENCE

Unlike a criminal case, in which a jury must find the defendant innocent if there is a reasonable doubt of his guilt, in a civil case the plaintiff must prove that the defendant was responsible for the accident and the damage that flowed directly from his or her act "by a fair preponderance of the credible evidence." Matters of negligence are usually tried before juries, although probably close to 95 percent of such cases are settled sometime before trial.

Often, however, negligence becomes a matter of a duty that has been imposed by statute: for instance, obeying traffic laws. If you are involved in an automobile accident and you have disobeyed one of these laws—for example, by going through a red light—you are presumed to be negligent and the plaintiff will most likely recover.

In rare instances, the simple fact that an accident occurred is enough to prove that someone was negligent. In law, this is called the doctrine of *res ipsa loquitur,* which literally translated means, "the thing speaks for itself." This doctrine applies only in cases in which the person who caused the accident had exclusive control over the instrument that caused the damage, the victim did nothing to contribute to the accident, and the accident would not normally have occurred unless someone was negligent.

The traditional example used in law school to illustrate this doctrine is the case of a man walking down the street just as a barrel of flour rolled out a window above a shop. It landed on him and he was seriously injured. The victim could not prove exactly how or why the barrel fell from the window, and the shopowner refused to admit any fault. The court ruled that because under normal circumstances this kind of accident would not have occurred unless someone was negligent, and since the owner of the store had the means to find out why the accident happened, it was up to him to prove that he was not negligent.

The doctrine of res ipsa loquitur would also apply if, for example, you entered a hospital to have your left leg amputated and upon waking up after the operation found that your right leg had been removed. In this case, the law would presume negligence on the part of the surgeon, the hospital, or both for amputating the wrong leg.

NEGLIGENCE DEFENSES

If you are the victim of an accident and are considering suing someone for negligence in causing that accident, there are several defenses that he might make, including the fact that you yourself might also have been negligent to some degree, or that you may have willingly assumed the risk involved in the act that caused the accident.

Other than simply denying fault, the following are the available defenses to negligence.

Contributory Negligence

In the past, every state followed the doctrine of contributory negligence. This meant that if your actions in any way contributed to causing the accident, you would not be compensated for your injuries unless you could show that the defendant acted intentionally or with "reckless" misconduct. For example, suppose that you were driving along a street with a posted speed limit of thirty-five miles per hour, but you were going fifty. To make matters worse, it was a rainy day and the roads were slick. A car ran a stop sign and hit you. You then sued the other driver. The defendant, however, could claim that you contributed to the accident by speeding, and that if you had obeyed the posted speed limits, you would have seen him run the stop sign and the accident could have been avoided. If the jury believed this argument, you would be found contributorily negligent and you would not be compensated for your injuries.

Comparative Negligence

Since the doctrine of contributory negligence has often been deemed unduly harsh, most states have adopted what is referred to as comparative negligence. In those jurisdictions where the doctrine of comparative negligence is followed, your negligence would be weighed against the negligence of the other party and the damages you are entitled to recover would be reduced by the percentage of fault assigned to you.

The speeding case above can also be used to illustrate this rule. A jury might decide that by speeding under those wet conditions you were 25 percent at fault in the accident. The total damages are found to be $100,000. However, since you have been assigned 25 percent of the fault, your recovery would be reduced by that amount, which means that you would only receive $75,000.

Within the doctrine of comparative negligence there are two variations. In some states you may collect from the other party only as long as you were not *more* negligent than he or she was. So, if you were equally at fault, you would collect 50 percent (in the above case, $50,000). However, if the jury decided your fault amounted to 51 percent, you would not recover anything.

Other states have adopted what is called "pure" comparative negligence. In these states, you can recover whatever percentage of the damages the jury determines. If, in our example, the court decided that by driving a car fifteen miles over the speed limit in wet conditions you were 75 percent negligent, you could still recover 25 percent of your damages, or $25,000. Theoretically, even if the court decided that you were 99 percent at fault, you would still receive 1 percent of the amount awarded for your damages. (See the Appendix for the status of contributory and comparative negligence state by state.)

The Assumption of Risk

In most cases, if you have knowingly and voluntarily assumed the risk inherent in a particular action that caused an accident, you cannot sue the other person for negligence. For instance, let's assume it's winter and you are visiting a friend. During your visit a snow and ice storm hits the area. When it's time for you to leave, your friend tells you not to go out the front door because the steps are covered by ice and suggests that you use the side door where there are no steps. You say, "Don't worry. I'll be careful," and, against your friend's advice, you use the front door. You slip and fall on the steps and break your arm. In most jurisdictions, under the doctrine of the assumption of risk, because you were aware of the danger and still chose to go down those steps even though you could have gone out the side door and avoided any possible danger, you would, in all likelihood, not be able to collect damages.

Another example of assumption of risk is participation in a sport in which certain risks are inherent to the game. For instance, if you are playing football and you get tackled and break an arm, you may not sue the person who tackled you. On the other hand, if you are playing tennis and a fight breaks out and you are hit in the head with a racket, you may sue the person who hit you, since the assumption of risk does not cover any injury that was intentionally inflicted and not an inherent part of the game.

STATUTE OF LIMITATIONS

In order to ensure that legal actions are brought in a timely fashion, every state has enacted laws that control the time frame within which a lawsuit may be brought. As a result, the liability for damage caused by a negligent act does not last forever. The reason for this is primarily pragmatic, since it is difficult to try a case ten or fifteen years after the accident, when the memory of witnesses is vague and the facts of the case may be obscured by time.

Statutes of limitation differ not only from state to state, but also in regard to the kinds of lawsuits involved. In some states the statute of limitations for medical malpractice, suits against governmental agencies, and wrongful death actions is shorter than that for other types of personal injury cases. In general, however, the statute of limitations for personal injury cases is from one to three years, and the clock begins to run from the time of the accident and the consequent injury. There are occasional exceptions, but they are so rare that you should not count on them. When the statute of limitations expires on your case, you simply don't have a case anymore. If an attorney did try to bring the case to court, it would automatically be dismissed.

Thus, to establish grounds for a personal injury case, you must have received a significant injury and must be able to prove that the accident was caused by the negligence of someone else. And because of the statute of limitations, you must make that determination in a relatively short period of time.

CHAPTER TWO

HOW TO CHOOSE THE

RIGHT ATTORNEY

IF YOU ARE in an accident, the first thing you should do is seek medical attention for your injuries. The second thing, whether you are the victim or the one who caused the accident, is consult an attorney.

If you caused the accident and you do not carry insurance, you will need an attorney to advise you about how to protect your rights, as well as to represent you in any possible negligence action.

If you were the injured party and have grounds for legal action, you will have a hard time handling your case without an attorney. Without proper representation, you run the risk of making some serious and costly mistakes.

CHOOSING THE RIGHT ATTORNEY FOR YOUR CASE

Some attorneys are generalists who practice a variety of aspects of the law, from preparing wills to handling divorces. Others specialize in a particular facet of the law. When it comes to personal injury cases, our advice is to find an attorney who specializes in that area, or a firm that has a personal injury department set up to handle such cases.

Personal injury law can be rather complex, and it is to your advantage to have an attorney working for you who is experienced and knowledgeable in the field. On the most basic level, the personal injury specialist will know immediately whether your case meets all the criteria necessary for you to bring suit and collect damages. The attorney should also be able to determine quickly what needs to be done on your case. He should have an understanding of your injuries and treatment and perhaps can even help you in obtaining needed medical treatment. The attorney can also determine whether expert witnesses are needed.

Just as important, a good, experienced personal injury attorney will be able to evaluate the extent of the damages you may be able to collect. This knowledge is obviously necessary if there is a settlement offer. For instance, let's say you tripped over several boxes of shoes left carelessly stacked in the aisle of a local shoe store. You fell and broke your arm. Your attorney demands $25,000 for your injury. The insurance company for the store offers a settlement of $20,000. An experienced, knowledgeable attorney will know, as a result of tracking the recent history of similar cases in the jurisdiction, whether this is a fair compromise. Using this information, your attorney might advise you to take the settlement as a reasonable compromise and to avoid the risks, expense, and delay of a trial.

Another reason to hire an attorney who specializes in the personal injury field is that he will be well-versed in the various state laws concerning your case and how they interact. This is especially important if your case is one in which the person responsible for the accident is either underinsured or uninsured, or in a state that has enacted no-fault insurance laws. For instance, suppose that you were a passenger in a car involved in an accident. You were injured, and the driver of the car was underinsured, which means that his insurance policy will not cover all the damages. Under most circumstances, you would be forced to settle for the limit of what the driver's insurance policy would pay, or less. However, a knowledgeable personal injury attorney, aware of the relevant issues and well-prepared to ask the proper questions, would have found out whether you, the victim, owned a car. If you did, the attorney would have known that your own automobile policy might pay the rest of your damages with its underinsured motorist coverage.

There are other criteria you ought to be aware of in choosing the right attorney. On balance, it's usually better to hire a local attorney, one who is more likely to be aware of the most recent rulings in your jurisdiction and where it would be best to file your lawsuit. Another important consideration is whether the attorney has had trial experience. It is rather surprising how few attorneys have actually tried cases in their careers. Although somewhere in the neighborhood of 95 percent of personal injury actions are settled out of court, if your case stands a good chance of going to trial, you should be represented by an attorney who has experience litigating personal injury cases.

In addition, you should consider whether the attorney (or his firm) has the financial resources to take on your case. A personal injury action may take up to five years to resolve and it is the attorney or the firm that advances the money used for expenses during that time. Usually, the larger firms, those with greater financial resources, are more capable of handling these costs.

In short, a good personal injury attorney knows the field, knows what law applies, knows how issues *should* be resolved, knows how to evaluate and negotiate, and knows how to present the case to a jury, if necessary.

How to Find the Right Attorney

The best way to begin your search for the right attorney is by asking friends and associates for recommendations. Perhaps they have had personal injury cases and have been pleased with the way their attorneys handled them. Or they may have had other occasions to use an attorney and, though that attorney might not be a personal injury specialist, they might be able to refer you to someone who is.

The Martindale Hubbell Law Directory, available in most law and public libraries, might be of some limited help. It is arranged geographically and covers virtually every large community in the country. Besides offering basic information, it sometimes lists the attorney's specialties and gives a brief resume. For the most part, however, this book is used by attorneys to find other attorneys, since it is difficult for a layman to get much useful information from such a technical source. Other available resources include the *Lawyer's Register by Specialties and Fields of Law,* along with various regional directories. You can also refer to your local Yellow Pages, which will give you an indication of the listed attorneys' areas of practice.

National or local bar associations will provide you with a list of attorneys. You should be aware, however, that bar associations do not make recommendations, so these lists should not be used as anything more than a starting point.

Many attorneys, including Jacoby & Meyers, advertise either in print or on television. This is another method of obtaining information on the availability of attorneys and their specialties. However, you should always investigate the credentials of these attorneys by asking for more information about their firm or speaking to them personally.

THE CONSULTATION

Once you have narrowed your list of attorneys to a few candidates, it's a good idea to schedule appointments with each of them. Personal injury attorneys will not charge for a consultation.

At the initial meeting be prepared to give an explanation of your accident. Bring along any documentation you have, including traffic collision reports, insurance information, medical records, photographs, and a list of possible witnesses. Try not to embellish and, most important, *do not lie.* Suppose, for instance, that you injured your arm in an accident and you tell your attorney that you had never injured it before. When the defendant's attorney checks and finds that you had a previous arm injury, your credibility and very possibly your case will be seriously jeopardized, since your attorney must then prove that your injury was a result of the second accident, not the first.

After describing your case you may want to ask the attorney a series of questions. For example:

- How long have you or your firm been in practice?
- What kinds of cases do you or your firm handle?
- Is your firm adequately organized to handle my kind of case?
- Do you think I have a feasible case, and if so will you handle it?
- How soon do you think you can begin working on my case?
- How long do you think my case might take to complete?
- Have you handled cases similar to mine and, if so, how many, and what results did you achieve?
- How do you intend to keep me informed of the progress of my case?
- How will you compute your contingency fees?

Even if you get satisfactory answers to these questions, the most important factor in your decision to hire an attorney will probably be your gut feelings. Was the attorney interested, attentive, knowledgeable, and informative? Was he organized and did he conduct the interview in a businesslike manner? Did he ask relevant questions? How did he relate to you personally? The rapport you have with your attorney is very important. If he appears to be distracted, bored, or short with you, you should probably look elsewhere. The chances are that you are going to have a long-term relationship with an attorney who represents you in a personal injury case, and you want to be able to relate well to him.

A Clients' Bill of Rights

Some years ago, at Jacoby & Meyers, we created a "Bill of Rights for Clients." This document grew out of our concern that our attorneys be client-oriented. In fact, what many attorneys think is good for the client is, in the opinion of the client, wrong eight times out of ten. Instead, what the client wants most—even more than results, although surely the client wants results—is a clear demonstration of concern and communication. The client wants to know that the attorney has his best interests at heart, and that the attorney is working *for him.*

With this in mind, we came up with the following doctrine:

1. All clients have the right to receive copies of paperwork and telephone calls, as well as periodic status reports from the attorney representing them, or someone working in the office who is familiar with their case.
2. All clients have the right during discussions to their attorney's full and exclusive attention, without interruptions, especially telephone interruptions.
3. All clients have the right to have their calls returned before the end of the business day, or at the longest within twenty-four hours.
4. All clients have the right to tell their attorneys what they want from them, to suggest how they can get it, and to have their attorneys proffer advice based on that right.
5. All clients have the right to be treated in a businesslike manner, including a full explanation of fees in the first consultation and regular billing and regular accounting of expenses.
6. All clients have the right to know how their attorneys intend to reach their goals, the options that are open to them, and the efforts their attorneys intend to make.
7. All clients have the right to be treated with respect and dignity—and that starts with a friendly smile from the receptionist and up-to-date periodicals in the waiting area.
8. All clients have the right to expect their attorneys to be good and sympathetic listeners—even though they may have heard the story three hundred times before from three hundred different clients.

9. All clients have the right to feel that their attorneys are indeed working for them.
10. All clients have the right to good, sound legal work.

You cannot know, of course, when choosing an attorney if he will respect your rights as a client. But it is certainly a good idea to keep these standards of professional conduct in mind when you make your choice, and insist upon them in your relationship with the attorney who is representing you.

FEES

One of the most unusual—and beneficial—aspects of a personal injury case is that the fees are customarily based on a percentage of the recovery; that is, the amount of the damages you are able to collect. This is called a *contingent fee,* which means that the attorney must win the case for you, either by an out-of-court settlement or a jury verdict, or he or she gets no fee.

The contingent fee rate ranges anywhere from 25 to 40 percent. In rare cases it might even go as high as 50 percent. The most common rate is 33 percent. Generally, the percentage is based on the nature and difficulty of the case and the experience and expertise of the attorney and his or her staff. The benefit of this arrangement is that you can truly feel that both you and your attorney are a team. It will not cost you any money to have the attorney represent you. He is gambling that he can help you recover for your injuries, and if he does he will share in the recovery as his compensation.

In cases against the federal government, as well as some states, there are statutory maximum limits on the percentage that an attorney may charge as a contingent fee. For instance, in personal injury suits filed against the United States government, the Federal Tort Claims Act places a limit of 20 percent on the fee if the case is settled before suit is filed and a 25 percent limit on the fee after suit is filed.

EXPENSES

During the course of the case, your attorney will probably advance payment for necessary expenses. These may include charges for such items as police reports, hospital reports, doctors' records, expert witness fees, and court filing fees. If the case is lost, the attorney may still be entitled to reimbursement of these charges, depending on the terms of employment. But as a practical matter, the attorney rarely collects for these expenses. In most instances, if the case is settled or won, the attorney's fee is a percentage of the amount of the full settlement, and costs and expenses are deducted from the client's share. In some instances, however, the attorney's fee is taken from the amount of the award minus the expenses.

For example, let's say your attorney charges a one-third contingent fee. He wins your case and an award of $100,000. During the course of the action expenses amount to $4,667. The breakdown of fees and expenses would be as follows:

Total amount of settlement	$100,000
Attorney's one-third share	$33,333
Costs and expenses	$4,667
Client's share before costs and expenses	$66,667
Client's share after costs and expenses	$62,000

It's a good idea to insist that your attorney provide you with a written fee agreement when he or she takes on your case. In some states, this is a requirement. And you may want to ask periodically what expenses have been incurred on your behalf.

WILL THE ATTORNEY TAKE YOUR CASE?

Basically, there are two business reasons why an attorney might refuse to take your case. The first is that in the attorney's opinion you don't have a feasible case, either because the criteria for liability have not been fulfilled, or because, due to your own contributory or comparative negligence or for some other reason, the likelihood of success is too small.

The other reason is economic. The attorney must determine whether the damage you incurred is serious enough to warrant accepting the case. The greater the damage, the larger the recovery and the attorney's fee. Also, the more complicated the case, the more serious the damage must be in order to make it an economically feasible case for an attorney to handle.

For instance, suppose that you tripped and fell over a bicycle left negligently on the sidewalk in the dark. You sprained your ankle, which necessitated a trip to the doctor and a loss of two days' work. If your case has a value of $1,500 in settlement or trial, your attorney's share would come to no more than $500, exclusive of the expenses involved in handling the case, and it might not be worth the time and effort it would take.

This doesn't mean that if you aren't injured seriously enough to recover for more than $5,000, you won't be able to find an attorney to handle your case. At Jacoby & Meyers, for instance, because of the unique way we are organized, we are able to take on many of the smaller cases, as well as the larger ones, that other attorneys cannot accept.

If you can't find an attorney to handle your case, this doesn't mean that all is lost. When the amount you feel you are entitled to recover is relatively small, you may take your case to small claims court. The maximum monetary limit on cases heard in this court varies from state to state, but it is usually at least $1,500.

HOW A CASE IS VALUED

One of the most troubling obstacles personal injury attorneys must deal with today is the public's misconception regarding the value of accident cases. The huge awards always make the headlines. They are, however, not only few and far between but are very often reduced either on appeal or through a negotiated settlement following the verdict. A negotiated settlement is a tactic employed to avoid going through a long appeal process and enables the plaintiff to receive his money more promptly.

Nevertheless, some people have an unrealistic notion of the amount of money they may obtain from a lawsuit. The huge awards, in fact, comprise only a small percentage of the cases adjudicated or settled each year. In fact, in a nation of 240 million people, there have been under two thousand awards of one million dollars or more in the last eighteen years. And in about two thirds of these cases, the victims suffered such serious injuries (brain damage, permanent paralysis, etc.) that they were in no shape to enjoy the spoils. Furthermore, you aren't likely to read about the thousands of cases that are taken to trial and lost by the injured party. In reality, most successful cases, including perhaps 90 percent of all successful personal injury claims, tend to result in a $7,500 to $20,000 recovery (of course, figures will vary in different jurisdictions).

The most important factors taken into account when evaluating a personal injury case are:

- The type of injury.
- The frequency, severity, and duration of pain resulting from the injury.
- The nature of any permanent residuals from the injury.
- The length of treatment.
- The cost of medical care.
- The extent of loss of earnings due to the injury.

Once these factors have been assessed, an experienced attorney will have a pretty good idea of what those injuries are worth in damages. For instance, there are benchmark value amounts for broken bones and what are known as soft-tissue injuries, which include strains and sprains.

The amount of lost earnings the victim has suffered is a particularly important factor in evaluating a personal injury case. For instance, suppose that two people are passengers in a car involved in an accident. The driver of the other car is at fault. Both victims suffer broken arms. However, one is a surgeon while the other works as an office manager. The amount of damages awarded to each will undoubtedly reflect the difference in their incomes. The surgeon will probably be awarded a larger settlement because his earning power is greater than that of the office manager and part of the settlement is supposed to replace the earnings the victim loses due to the accident.

According to some attorneys yet another subtle factor limiting the size of recoveries is the state of the economy. Traditionally, they maintain, in times of recession the courts have restricted the right to sue by limiting the grounds on which people can rely to make their case. In other words, as the economy worsens the courts opt for a more narrow construction of the law in personal injury cases.

PREDICTING SETTLEMENTS

Among the first questions a client usually asks an attorney is "How much do you think my case is worth?" Unfortunately, this is an unanswerable question and you should probably be wary of any attorney who answers it with a precise figure or makes predictions or promises about the recovery you will get before he has had an opportunity to review all the relevant information.

For one thing, in most cases no one can immediately tell how seriously you have been injured. By their very nature, some injuries don't manifest themselves until long after an accident. For this reason you should refrain from signing any kind of release immediately after an accident.

Thus, it is always a good idea to contact an attorney as soon as possible after you have been injured, since it is the attorney who can advise you of your rights as well as inform you of the proper procedures, which include seeing the doctors in the appropriate specialties to evaluate and treat your type of injury.

One of the more irritating experiences faced by attorneys is the client who comes in, tells the attorney about his case and then announces, "My friend Joe had the very same accident I had and his injuries were pretty much the same as mine. He got $50,000, so that's what I expect to get." Sounds reasonable, but is it true? Absolutely not. Every case is different and must be evaluated on the basis of the specific facts of that case. There are always different facts, and any slight variation might cause an enormous difference in recovery.

Another factor that causes apparent inconsistencies in recoveries is the difference in the jurisdictions in which cases are brought. In some jurisdictions the juries are more liberal in their awards; in others they are far more conservative. Also, if the case does make it to trial, the parties will be facing a jury, which might or might not be sympathetic to either the plaintiff or the defendant. In short, there are just too many variables to allow one to compare personal injury cases and their recoveries easily. No one case will match yours exactly, and nobody knows what your case will be worth until it has been investigated and evaluated carefully. That is the job of the skilled, experienced personal injury attorney, and all the more reason for you to find one as soon as possible after you suffer an accident.

CHAPTER THREE

FOLLOWING YOUR CASE

IN MANY WAYS the workings of the law are obvious and yet, at the same time, somewhat mysterious. All of us have grown up watching courtroom dramas on television and in the movies, we have read about legal cases in novels and nonfiction books, magazines and newspapers. We have seen, although only to a limited extent, how a legal case is built, shaped, then brought into the courtroom and argued. We have even, in films like *Twelve Angry Men,* witnessed how a jury works. In short, the law has proved fertile ground for the dramatic imagination.

But as much as we may think we know about the law, most layman understand surprisingly little about the nitty-gritty, day-to-day workings of the legal profession. Ironically, some clients prefer it this way, as do some attorneys. Clients often place blind faith in those who represent them, and those who represent them sometimes play on this blind faith, since it allows them carte blanche in the manner in which they function.

However, some of us in the legal profession believe that demystifying the law is in the best interests not only of the client but also of the attorney. The more you, as a client, know about how the law works, the better you can aid your attorney. The same goes for communication between attorney and client. As long as the lines of communication remain open, there is less chance of misunderstandings that can lead to hard feelings and resentment.

Some might argue that too much knowledge can create a dangerous situation in the relationship between client and attorney. In fact, it could promote unnecessary and conceivably destructive interference on the part of the client, which may create problems for an attorney and ultimately for the client. However, at Jacoby & Meyers we believe that the more clients know about the workings of the law, the easier it is for us to represent them effectively. And if a client understands how and at what pace a case proceeds, he or she is less likely to make frequent and unnecessary calls to check on the case.

One of the most common complaints made by clients about their attorneys is "I don't know what's going on. My lawyer never talks to me." This is a valid grievance and it is one that can drive a wedge between attorney and client that may work to the detriment of the successful resolution of the case.

Once an attorney has agreed to handle your case, it's perfectly proper to call him after two to four weeks to see what kind of progress is being made. Thereafter, if you don't receive periodic update letters or calls from your attorney or his staff, it's not unreasonable to call every month or so to see how things are going. But remember, the progress of a personal injury case can be frustratingly slow, and many relevent issues depend upon the cooperation and participation of people other than your attorney (medical personnel, witnesses, and the opposing attorneys, for example). So you must be patient. A good attorney, however, will make sure that he is on top of the case, and will make every effort to keep you fully informed.

Let's examine how an attorney will most likely proceed, before litigation, in the average personal injury action. By understanding these procedures you will become a more informed and helpful client, better able to communicate effectively with your attorney.

SETTLING OUT OF COURT

For several reasons it is almost always in the best interest of the client to reach an early settlement of a personal injury case before embarking upon litigation. For one thing, litigation is costly. It is also time consuming, and the process, which includes the taking of testimony (depositions) and the hostilities that are bound to ensue, is a stressful one. Because of the time and expense involved, prolonged litigation can take a heavy emotional toll on those involved.

In the majority of cases that involve smaller amounts of money—that is, cases in which the injuries are not catastrophic and the recovery will not be significant—many attorneys will try to settle before instituting litigation proceedings. This makes sense, since the costs of litigating such an action might be larger than the potential recovery. On the other hand, in cases that involve much larger amounts, there is less likelihood of a quick settlement and the attorney may have to begin a lawsuit early on in order to obtain a justifiable award for the client.

STEP ONE: RETAINER AND AUTHORIZATIONS

After you've selected your attorney and he has agreed to represent you, the first thing you will be asked to do is sign a retainer agreement. This agreement will set forth the ground rules for the fee you will be expected to pay, which will include the contingent fee percentage as well as the method to be employed to deduct the expenses and costs from your recovery.

At the time you sign the retainer agreement, you will also be asked to sign a set of authorizations that will allow your attorney to obtain information on your behalf. This would include any medical and police reports that are required to investigate your case.

Now that you are represented by an attorney, it is imperative that you refer all matters pertaining to your case to your attorney. If people contact you concerning the accident, take their names and numbers and tell them that your attorney will get in touch with them, or refer them directly to your attorney. You should follow this procedure even with your own insurance carrier. It is your attorney's job to deal with these matters.

STEP TWO: GATHERING INFORMATION

Once you have signed the retainer agreement and applicable authorizations, your attorney will begin to gather information pertaining to your case. During this stage of the action one of the questions most commonly asked by the client is "Who else is going to know about my case?"

The answer is:

- Your insurance carrier.
- The defendant and his attorney and insurance carrier.
- The police.
- The photographer and investigator (if necessary) assigned to the case by your attorney.
- Your health-care provider (doctors, hospitals, or both).
- Witnesses.
- Your employer, if you are claiming damages for lost earnings.
- Other members of your attorney's firm.

In the typical automobile accident case, the first thing your attorney will do is obtain a traffic collision report (otherwise referred to as a police report) from the police. It will describe the circumstances of the accident and name all the parties involved. Any possible witnesses, whose names either were provided by you or appear in the police report, will be contacted by your attorney. Concurrently, in order to obtain records of your medical treatment and lost wages, your attorney will contact your doctor, the hospital where you were treated (if hospital treatment was necessary), and your employer. Although the wheels can be set into motion immediately regarding collection of this information, in most instances your case can't actually begin to be settled or tried until your treatment has been completed. If treatment might be spread out over a number of years, the action can begin immediately and experts will be used to determine the likely cost of long-term care. Your attorney will also contact the insurance carriers involved, putting them on notice that you, the victim of the accident, now have legal representation.

If you have been involved in an automobile accident in a no-fault state, your attorney will obtain a no-fault application in order to submit all of your medical bills for payment and obtain other benefits, which include compensation for lost earnings. Your attorney will also provide the defendant's insurance carrier with authorizations to obtain your medical records and your salary records if lost wages are claimed, and with information concerning your legal claims against their insured. Since a quick, amicable settlement is always preferable to prolonged litigation, your attorney should give the insurance carrier a reasonable period of time to gather from doctors and employers the information necessary to verify the extent of your injuries and damages. But that period should not be unnecessarily prolonged.

While your attorney gets the ball rolling, he should also make certain that you are receiving the appropriate medical treatment. Naturally, it is your responsibility to obtain the best possible medical treatment from a doctor who specializes in treating your type of injury. There is, however, a difference of opinion about whether attorneys should refer their clients to particular doctors at some later time. Many attorneys frown on this practice, since it may appear that they are pushing their client into treatment. They may wish to avoid any problem that might arise if the doctor they suggested fails to provide the proper treatment. Other attorneys feel that they are providing a necessary service to those clients who are simply unable to find an appropriate doctor. In some cases, they may also wish to obtain further verification from a specialist of the nature and extent of your injuries and the cost of treatment. In such cases, your attorney might offer a list of physicians he considers competent. In general, however, you should avoid attorneys who insist upon your seeing "their" physician.

In our experience, the average time of treatment for soft-tissue injuries such as strains and sprains is six months or less.

If you are the victim of such an injury, communication between you, your doctor, and your attorney is very important during this period. Cooperation helps move the case along. As your treatment progresses, you should make sure that your attorney receives periodic reports on your progress from your doctor. Also, your attorney should be apprised of any significant changes in your health. All injuries must be documented. A doctor simply *telling* you or your attorney that there are injuries is not enough. Your attorney should also be immediately notified upon the completion of your treatment. Once your medical treatment is concluded, your attorney will send your doctor a request for the final bill and medical report. Only when this information is obtained can the next stage of your case begin.

If you are the victim of a more serious accident, you may miss a good deal of work. During this time money may be scarce and in some cases accident victims are forced to return to work before their doctors find they are physically able to do so. When money is scarce, some clients may ask their attorneys for help, perhaps seeking a small loan to tide them over. After all, they reason, this is just another expense and when the case is finally settled the attorney can simply add the loan to expenses.

On the face of it this sounds reasonable. However, ethical rules prohibit an attorney from advancing or loaning money to a client in almost every state. The reason is simple: The attorney who advances or loans money to a client might, in effect, be purchasing an interest in the lawsuit. Ethically, an attorney is supposed to have only the best interests of his client in mind. If the attorney's own money is "invested" in the lawsuit, he may make a decision that instead of being in the client's best interests is only in the attorney's best interests. Loaning money to a client may create an inappropriate relationship (or a conflict of interest) between client and attorney, which could have a serious impact on the attorney's professional judgment.

For this reason clients should scrupulously avoid attorneys who offer to loan them money. If you are in need of money, borrow it elsewhere. If you are forced to return to work earlier than medically advisable, it may not hurt your action as long as you get a note from your doctor stating that he believes it is unwise to return to work at that point in your medical recovery. If it's simply a matter of paying a doctor's bill, your attorney should send the physician what is known as a letter of protection, which is a promise to pay the bill as soon as the case is completed. This allows the physician to have a lien on the case, should he choose to accept that in lieu of immediate payment.

On the average, it takes two or three weeks to get responses from doctors and to obtain police reports, if the accident was reported to police. In some cases, however, it may take substantially longer. In New York, for instance, it can take up to six to ten weeks to obtain a police report. Consequently, your attorney's progress may be delayed somewhat by events beyond his control.

STEP THREE: THE INVESTIGATION

Once most of the initial information has been gathered, your attorney will begin the investigation of the accident. It's always in the best interests of the client to investigate as soon as possible, since evidence may later be harder to obtain and memories may begin to fade.

Your attorney will speak to witnesses and get their statements, as well as photographs of the vehicle (if it was an automobile accident), and sometimes even the scene of the accident. Often, the client is asked to provide these photographs, if possible, to cut down on costs. You, as the client, should also provide your attorney with relevent information, such as addresses and phone numbers, thereby cutting investigation time and expenses.

Your attorney will try to determine the amount of insurance available; that is, the amount of coverage the person deemed responsible for the accident carries in the form of automobile or homeowner's insurance. Attorneys are entitled to learn this information when the case is actually in litigation. Otherwise they must use various other means to try to obtain this figure, and sometimes it cannot be obtained.

At this time your attorney will also examine and assess the extent of your injuries. There are several categories of injury cases we see regularly.

1. *Soft-tissue injuries.* These are the most common accidental injuries, and they include sprains and muscle or ligament strains. Most often they occur in automobile accidents, in which whiplash is the most common injury, and in slip and fall accidents. Treatment for these injuries can range from a few days to several weeks or months. Depending upon their seriousness, soft-tissue injuries often fall into a predictable range for settlements, because they are very common and both attorneys and insurance companies have a good deal of experience with such cases.

2. *Fractures.* These are broken bones, which may be either "simple" or "compound" fractures. The particular bones that are broken may influence the range of recovery. For instance, a broken leg may be "worth" more than broken ribs, because someone with broken ribs may be able to return to his or her job while the injury is still healing. Someone who has broken a leg may not be able to work at all.

3. *Injuries to discs.* These are injuries that damage the spinal bones of either the neck or the back, and they usually result in either bulging or herniated discs in the spine, which may affect a spinal nerve. Sometimes, these injuries require surgery or prolonged periods of bed rest. The seriousness of the injury, the medical treatment necessary, and the ensuing convalescent period all bear heavily on the range of recovery. There is a wide range of possible recoveries for these injuries, as well as a wide range of jury verdicts or out-of-court settlements.

. . .

4. *Scarring.* Generally, facial scarring brings a higher recovery than scars that are, under normal circumstances, unseen. By the same token, facial scarring on a young person or a female will probably bring a larger recovery than the same scarring on an older person or a male. The potential for surgical revision of scars, and the effect on the victim of having the scars, are major factors in the amount of recovery.

5. *Amputations.* These may be minor amputations, such as portions of toes or fingertips, or major amputations, such as entire limbs. The verdict or settlement value of these cases depends not only on the individual injury and the pain that accompanies that injury, but also on the victim's age, sex, occupation, and marital status. In major amputation cases, physical and emotional suffering figures highly into any recovery, as well as the likelihood that the victim can return to work.

6. *Catastrophic injuries.* These are injuries that result in paralyzation, such as paraplegia (both lower limbs paralyzed) and quadriplegia (both lower and upper limbs paralyzed). Often these injuries are the result of severe spinal cord damage. They are most prevalent in automobile, motorcycle, and diving accidents. Cases involving these injuries generally result in very large awards, since lost wages and medical expenses, as well as pain and suffering, can be overwhelming. Additionally, there are often lifetime medical treatment expenses and continuing wage loss, both of which are figured into any settlement.

7. *Psychological damage.* These injuries arise as a direct result of physical damages. Cases involving this type of claim are becoming more prevalent as medical science explores the relationship between psychological damage and physical injuries.

Psychological damages require medical or professional treatment in order to make them part of any claim.

8. *Brain damage.* Injuries to the brain can sometimes cause total incapacity, or sometimes affect only certain body functions. In some cases, these injuries lead to huge damage awards.

9. *Wrongful death.* Death that occurs as the result of someone's negligent actions (or inaction) may also result in large damage awards.

After obtaining all the pertinent information about the exact nature and extent of your injury, the costs of treatment and recuperation and other relevant factors, your attorney will determine the amount of damages he will seek, determine the liability and coverage of the person deemed responsible for the accident, and estimate a range of value for your case. Any attorney who attempts to place a value of your case before he has all this information should be suspect, since without extensive investigation there is really no way to be sure how much a case is worth. Avoid any attorney who makes an off-the-cuff promise concerning the amount of money you will get.

At this point in your case, your attorney will send what is known as a "demand letter" to the insurance company describing the defendant's liability and your damages. If liability and damages are clear-cut, the case may be settled quickly. However, if your medical treatment is not complete, you should probably wait to settle, unless, of course, treatment will be long-term.

STEP FOUR: SETTLEMENT

If liability is clearly established and accepted by the defendant's insurance carrier, a settlement offer will be made. Be advised, however, that this offer may not come quickly. Insurance companies are like dinosaurs: They are big and they are slow. The demand letter might sit on an insurance adjustor's desk for a week or two before even being read. Then it must be evaluated by the adjustor. And remember, the adjustor's job is to try to minimize or avoid paying claims. He will look for a way out, either in liability or in damages, or in both, if possible. After the adjustor evaluates the claim and decides to settle, the settlement offer must then be approved by the insurance company. Again, since there are usually many levels in the company hierarchy, this adds to the amount of time you will have to wait. You shouldn't be surprised if the entire procedure takes up to two months. However, attorneys can speed the process by providing the adjustor with all the proper documents and by maintaining a good relationship with that adjustor.

Once the settlement offer is received by your attorney, it is his duty to inform you of it and advise you whether, in his opinion, it is a fair settlement. Ultimately, however, the decision to accept or reject the offer is yours and yours alone.

If you believe that the settlement offer is too low, your attorney will try to negotiate a higher settlement. Negotiations can take months. Your attorney may or may not be successful in raising the offer. When he advises you that he has obtained the best offer he can get for your case, you must, once again, decide whether to take the settlement offer. One thing to remember in making that decision is that a settlement offer is a compromise in which both sides have to give up something. If everyone is unhappy, this probably means it is a reasonable compromise and the offer should be accepted.

As we mentioned before, one of the biggest mistakes clients make is comparing their settlement offer to the settlement obtained by someone else in a similar case. Again, every case has its own unique facts and must be judged on its own merits. As for the time within which the average negotiated settlement (that is, one that is reached before any litigation is instituted) is reached, you can usually figure on two to six months from the time medical treatment ends, although it can be sooner, or, in some instances, it can even take as long as two years.

STEP FIVE: OBTAINING YOUR SETTLEMENT

There are several steps you and your attorney must take to receive payment of your settlement.

1. A release must be signed by the client, absolving the defendant of any further liability.
2. This release must be forwarded to the insurance carrier.
3. A check is then made out to the client and the client's law firm by the insurance company and sent to the attorney.
4. After the check is received, it is signed by both the attorney and the client and the check is deposited in an escrow account.
5. The check is cleared by the bank.
6. From the escrow account, the attorney is entitled to withdraw the agreed-upon percentage of the settlement as his fee, in addition to any expenses incurred in handling your case, which should be fully documented for your inspection.
7. The attorney issues a check for the balance in the escrow account to the client.

Under normal circumstances this process can take up to six weeks. However, there are several steps that can be taken to speed things along. First, the client may come into the attorney's office to sign the release, rather than doing it through the mail. Next, the client may sign a power of attorney, giving the attorney the right to endorse the settlement check issued by the insurance company. This saves another trip to the office in order to coendorse the check. And finally, the client may come into the office to pick up the final check, rather than have it mailed. If these time-saving procedures are followed, many settlements may be obtained within three or four weeks. But you should remember that there are always exceptions. For instance, if you're dealing with a governmental defendant, it will inevitably take longer.

It is, in a majority of cases, to the client's advantage to accept a settlement for reasons of both common sense and dollars and cents. If it is fair and reasonable compensation for your injury, it is only common sense to take it and put the matter behind you. If you believe the compensation is not fair, you will have to take the next step in the process—litigation—which is expensive and offers no guarantee that you will win a larger award. In fact, given the time required and the unpredictability and stress of the litigation process, settling a case is sometimes the best route to take.

CHAPTER FOUR

LITIGATION

ALTHOUGH SOME ATTORNEYS do have the knee-jerk tendency to sue immediately without trying to settle, the vast majority will attempt to get fair value for your case without running the risk of spending up to five years in litigation and ultimately losing the case. The fact is, many personal injury cases are settled before any court action, and only about 5 percent go to trial. However, if you fail to reach a settlement with the defendant or the defendant's insurance carrier, your attorney will probably begin litigation. Basically, an attorney will begin litigation for any one or a combination of three reasons.

1. The case is too large in terms of money value to be settled quickly.
2. There is a major dispute about liability (the facts of the case—for example who was really responsible for the injury—are in question.
3. The two parties cannot agree on a negotiated settlement.

The information that follows is a general rundown of the litigation process from the filing of the complaint through the trial, appeal, and collection of judgment.

WAYS TO LITIGATE

In most jurisdictions there are three basic ways to litigate.

1. In more serious cases, generally those in which the recovery amount is over $25,000 (depending upon the jurisdiction), the plaintiff may demand a jury trial. However, in most jurisdictions this may result in the passing of several years before your case will be heard. Unlike television shows in which cases seem to come to court almost immediately and are wrapped up in an hour's time, the reality is much less immediate. Some states, such as Arizona, actually have rules ensuring that cases make it to court within two years. But in other jurisdictions, such as the New York and Philadelphia areas, there may be up to a five-year wait before a case actually comes to trial. Of course, you may settle the case at any time during this waiting period, as well as during the trial or even after the trial has been completed.

2. If you are suing for an amount under $25,000 (again, depending upon the jurisdiction), you may choose to go to an arbitration hearing. In some jurisdictions, it is required that you go to such a hearing. Depending upon the rules of the jurisdiction in which you bring the case, your action will be heard by anywhere from one to three attorneys. The advantage to this choice of forum is that your case will probably take only nine months or so to be heard. Generally, by choosing arbitration you don't give up your opportunity to appeal the decision. In California, for instance, if you reject the arbitrator's decision, you may proceed to trial.

3. If you would rather not have a jury trial or go to arbitration, you may take advantage of a private court system, which is sort

of a minientrepreneurial answer to the clogged public court system. In this procedure both sides agree on a private adjudicator, usually a retired judge. In electing this option, you waive your right to a jury trial. However, you will considerably shorten the time involved, since in most cases there is no more than a two- or three-month wait. If you do choose the private court system, there is a minor expense involved in hiring the adjudicator (the plaintiff pays), which is almost always offset by the speed of the process.

If your case goes to a jury trial, it will generally progress through the litigation process in the following steps. Of course, every jurisdiction, and to some extent every individual court, has its own procedures and idiosyncracies (the federal court system, however, is more uniform). In addition, time periods vary from place to place.

STEP ONE: THE PLEADING

The Complaint

The first phase of any lawsuit is called the pleading stage and it generally begins with the attorney for the plaintiff filing a complaint in court. The complaint lists the plaintiff's claim in some detail (statements of how an accident happened, for example, and what injuries were caused), while also stating the cause or causes of action (the legal grounds for the claim).

The clerk of the court then issues a summons to the defendant. The summons names the plaintiff and defendant, as well as the court to which the defendant is summoned to answer the complaint. It also specifies the time the defendant is given to file an answer (usually from twenty to thirty days) and where this answer must be filed.

The next step is to serve the summons and complaint on the defendant. Your attorney will do this either by hand delivery executed by the marshal's office, a professional process server, a member of the attorney's staff, or mail. This last method is generally used only when the defendant is represented by an attorney who has agreed to accept the summons and complaint on behalf of his client, or in some states where the rules permit service by mail, or when the defendant is out of the jurisdiction of the court.

The Answer

Once the summons and complaint have been received by the defendant or his attorney, an answer must be filed with the clerk of the court. The answer may include one or more of the following (again, this procedure may vary from state to state):

- A general denial of the claim, sometimes known as a demurrer.
- An allegation of an affirmative defense, which would include the introduction of new information meant to defeat the plaintiff's claim. This answer might admit that the accident occurred but denies that it was the defendant's fault.
- A counterclaim, which is a claim made by the defendant against the plaintiff to offset the plaintiff's claim. Often, when there are multiple defendants in a case, the answer of one defendant may include a crossclaim against another defendant. In essence, this means that Defendant A is alleging that the accident was the fault of Defendant B and that therefore Defendant A has no responsibility. For instance, suppose that you were in an automobile accident in which a truck swerved in front of you, and in your attempt to avoid colliding with the truck you hit another car. You are sued by the driver of that car and you, in turn, sue the driver of the truck, who caused the accident.

If the defendant simply ignores the complaint and summons and doesn't file an answer, the plaintiff's attorney can file for a "default." If a judge finds that the complaint and summons were properly served, that the time for answering the complaint has elapsed, and that the defendant was notified of the default hearing, the judge will probably grant the default. This will result in a judgment being entered against the defendant by the court, awarding the plaintiff damages.

A default judgment may be reversed only if the defendant acts promptly and can show some valid reason (such as illness, or that the summons and complaint were never actually served) for not responding to the complaint.

STEP TWO: DISCOVERY

Once the complaint and summons have been served and the answer filed, the discovery period begins. This is a process of formal and intensive investigation wherein each side gathers evidence to prepare and strengthen its own case. It is also a process through which both sides have the right to find out everything about their opponent's case. In some states pretrial examinations are mandatory, in others they are voluntary.

Discovery may be conducted in a variety of ways. Witnesses may be interviewed. Doctors may also be interviewed. Medical records may be subpoenaed and evaluated. The scene of the accident may be analyzed. Experts may be consulted and additional reports obtained.

Basically, the aim of discovery is to get to the truth by making sure that both sides have all the information concerning the facts of the incident. It is believed that justice is best served when there are no surprises at the time of the trial. Rather, each side should be aware of the other side's case and therefore prepared to offer strong counterarguments. The underlying assumption is that in this way the truth will eventually be arrived at. And once the facts have been uncovered, they can be presented to an impartial jury of peers to make the final decision. The discovery process can also serve to encourage settlement of the case before it goes to trial.

Interrogatories

During the discovery process, interrogatories are exchanged by the parties in the dispute to find out just what the facts are. Interrogatories are written questions posed by one side to the other, which are to be answered in affidavits, written statements made under oath. If the case concerns an automobile accident, questions to the defendant might include, "How fast were you driving?" "Had you had anything to drink?" "Was there anyone in the car with you?" "Had you had any problem with your brakes?" "What witnesses do you plan to call on your behalf?" The plaintiff may also ask the amount of the defendant's insurance coverage at this point.

Generally, depending upon the rules of the individual state, interrogatories must be submitted and answered between 30 and 180 days from the time the action is brought. Failure of a party to respond to interrogatories may result in sanctions, or heavy penalties by the court.

Depositions

Your attorney can also "depose" any participants in or witnesses to the accident. A deposition is oral testimony taken outside of court. During such testimony attorneys for both sides may ask questions of the opposing party or a witness for the other side. If you are asked to give a deposition, you will be sworn in and give your testimony under oath. The obligation to tell the truth is vital. If you are found to be lying while giving a deposition, you can be held guilty of the crime of perjury.

If you are the plaintiff, you will be deposed by the defendant's attorney; your attorney will depose the defendant. The advantage to a deposition over a written interrogatory is that the attorneys may ask follow-up questions, which allows them to put flesh and bones on the framework of the case stated in the complaint. Depositions can help make or break a settlement, since they allow the opposing attorneys to see, firsthand, just how strong the case is, and what kind of witnesses the plaintiff or the defendant will be at trial.

Under most circumstances, a deposition is taken in the office of the attorney who is administering it. However, an empty room in the courthouse or some other mutually agreed upon place may also be used. Attorneys for both the defendant and the plaintiff will be present. The proceedings are recorded by a court stenographer and the transcript may be used at the trial if a witness does not come to the trial, or to contradict the testimony of a witness if his story changes. Occasionally, depositions are videotaped, especially when it appears that a witness may not be able to testify at a trial because he will be out of state or due to advanced age or illness.

During the taking of a deposition, your attorney is usually permitted to make objections to questions put to you by the opposing attorney as well as to make attempts to clarify confusing questions. Before your deposition, your attorney should thoroughly brief you about the kinds of questions you may expect. If you have any questions about the procedure, don't hesitate to ask. Most often, your own attorney will not ask you any questions at all at your deposition, since he can talk to you at any time. But the opposing attorney normally only gets one opportunity to ask questions before trial.

Here are some tips on how to conduct yourself during the taking of a deposition:

- Make sure you fully understand any question before attempting to answer it. If you are confused, say so and ask that the question be rephrased or further explained.
- Don't volunteer any information. Rather, simply answer the questions that are put to you.
- Make sure that your responses are verbal. For instance, when asked about a particular injury, don't simply point to it, but name the place on your body that has been affected. Otherwise, your answer won't show up in the transcript, and it won't make any sense.

- Make sure your answer is clear, well thought out, spoken with authority, and most important, heard. Don't speak while someone else is speaking. If you do, your statement may be missed or garbled by the court stenographer.
- Don't improvise. If you're not sure of an answer to a question put to you, just say that you don't know. Remember, you are testifying under oath, and if you answer when you're not sure of the facts, you open yourself up to contradictions, which may be used against you later on in court. If you don't know the answer, don't guess. You're not expected to know everything.
- Don't answer a question over the objections of your attorney, but stop and wait until the objection is dealt with and duly noted, and only then, with the permission of your attorney, answer it. Some questions asked by the opposition may be inappropriate, meant only as a "fishing expedition" to uncover possible evidence for its side.
- Don't appear hostile or argumentative.
- Don't argue with the opposing attorney.
- Don't let the opposing attorney goad you into any statement that might be beneficial to the opposition's case.
- Think about the accident, your injuries, your treatment, and the other facts of the case before the deposition. You will remember more accurately if you have previously given these matters some thought.
- Be prepared and be sure your attorney is prepared.

Once the deposition has been transcribed, you will be given the opportunity to review it to make sure that your answers were accurate. At this time, you may make changes in the record, but later, when the case goes to trial, you may be asked to explain these changes and why you made them.

Because any answers that you give at a trial will be compared to those you gave in a deposition, it is very important that there be no contradictions. If there are, you can be sure that the opposition will use them against you. For this reason, you should be very careful about reviewing what you said to make sure that it was as accurate an answer as you are capable of giving.

You are also permitted to review your deposition before trial. This is almost always a good idea, because it can serve to refresh your memory of the facts, which, due to the passage of time between the accident and the trial, may have become somewhat faded.

Many witnesses may be deposed during the discovery process. Also often included in the discovery is a physical examination of the plaintiff by a doctor of the defendant's choosing, who may testify for the defendant at trial. Depending upon the complexity of a case, the number of parties involved, and the jurisdiction, the discovery process can take anywhere from six months to a year or more to be completed. However, during this phase of your case, it's a good idea to make sure that your attorney is moving matters along as quickly as possible. A phone call to check periodically on the progress of your case should do the trick.

STEP THREE: THE TRIAL

The Trial Date

After the discovery portion of the action is completed, your case will be placed on the court calendar, which is nothing more than a listing of dates on which the cases ready for trial will be heard. Depending upon the jurisdiction in which you reside, the court date you receive may be more than a year away, or in some cases, several years in the future.

It is in the best interests of the insurance companies to drag out a case as long as possible. In part, this is simply a wise business decision. They want to hold on to their money as long as they can. Once an action is brought, the insurance company immediately puts a sum of money on reserve and so, while the case drags on, they are receiving interest on this money. Although few cases run into the big awards we often read about, when you add up the number of small cases for which money is put aside, the interest figures become considerable.

Another reason it's in the insurance companies' interests to prolong a case is that they believe that time is their ally and the longer the case drags on the more likely it is that the plaintiff will be willing to settle for a smaller amount. And witnesses disappear or forget as time goes by, making the case more difficult.

For these reasons, and because there may be scheduling conflicts for both attorneys, a case seldom actually comes to trial on the original date set. Almost as a matter of course, opposing attorneys will ask for, and will usually be granted, a reasonable number of postponements.

However, there is always the possibility of a settlement being reached at any time during this long waiting period. Most cases are settled just as they are starting trial. Unfortunately, it often takes that long for both sides to assess the case fully and to come to an agreement on its value.

Pretrial Motions

During the months before trial your attorney may make what are called pretrial motions. These may include a motion for "summary judgment," which is an attempt to have the case decided by a judge before it actually goes to trial (either side may file this type of motion). A motion for summary judgment in favor of the defendant would usually be filed if the defendant's attorney believes that since there are no facts in dispute no one could reasonably question the defendant's right to win the case. A brief is filed outlining each side's arguments along with supporting evidence, which might include depositions and sworn affidavits. If the law and the evidence support it, the judge will grant the motion for summary judgment and there will not be a trial. However, if evidence provided shows that the facts could be determined either way by a jury, or that the plaintiff has the right to win, the judge will deny the motion.

The reason for this is that it is not up to the judge to decide what the facts of a case actually are; that is, who is telling the truth. This task is left up to a jury. It is very rare for a plaintiff to be granted summary judgment.

Before the trial your attorney or the attorney representing the other side may make a variety of motions concerning the applicable law in the case or the evidence that can be presented at trial. For example, the defendant may not have provided you with information that should be available to you. If this happens, your attorney will file a motion to force the defendant to provide this information. Because most pretrial motions are rather technical, you should ask your attorney to explain what they mean and what he hopes to achieve by their use.

The Pretrial Conference

Sometime just before your trial is scheduled to begin, the judge assigned to your case will call a pretrial conference to see if there is any possibility for a negotiated settlement and perhaps to determine if there are motions that may need to be decided before settlement can occur. The judge will often take an active role in trying to get the two sides to reach a negotiated settlement. For instance, he may suggest possible compromises by actually placing a dollar value on the case. If, after these attempts, a negotiated settlement does not appear to be possible, the case will be brought to trial.

Jury Selection

In some instances, either as a result of the agreement of both parties or due to statutory requirement, a personal injury case will be heard only by a judge. However, the vast majority of cases that go to trial are heard by a jury. Thus, the first step in a trial is usually the selection of that jury.

Initially, there is a panel of from twenty to several hundred men and women from which twelve, or in some cases, eight or six are selected to hear the case. These men and women are chosen from within the community. Their names are taken from either the voter registration rolls or other registration rolls, such as those compiled by the local motor vehicle department.

The process of actually choosing the jurors who will hear your case is called the *voir dire*. During the voir dire, attorneys for both sides will ask questions of prospective jurors aimed at finding and eliminating those who cannot be fair and impartial. Those jurors who display overt bias are challenged for cause and, if the judge agrees, they will be dismissed from service. Others may be dismissed without cause (peremptory challenges), simply because an attorney has a gut feeling that these prospective jurors would be biased against his client, no matter how unbiased they claim to be. Any number of prospective jurors may be challenged for cause, but only a certain number can be peremptorily challenged by each side. For this reason, a good attorney will exercise his peremptory challenges very carefully.

There is one exception to this voir dire procedure. Most federal judges (and some state judges) perform the voir dire questioning themselves, thereby eliminating attorneys from the selection process (although the attorneys are still permitted to challenge prospective jurors). However, this procedure has been under fire for some time and there are moves afoot to permit attorneys to perform voir dire questioning in federal cases as well. There is also a move in some states, California being one of them, to restrict voir dire by attorneys.

Once the jurors have been chosen (the number depends upon the jurisdiction in which the case is brought), along with one or two alternates selected in the event that one of the main jurors cannot perform his duty, they will take their place in the jury box and the trial begins with opening statements and the presentation of evidence from both sides. The duty of the jury is to decide among themselves which evidence is valid, who is telling the truth, and who is not. In other words, it is up to the jury to determine what the facts of the case really are. Once these facts have been established, it is the duty of the jury to apply these facts as they find them to the law as applicable to the particular case. The jury is instructed regarding what the law is by the judge.

The basic rule in a civil case is that the plaintiff must prove his case by a "fair preponderance of the evidence." Unlike a criminal trial, a civil trial places the burden of proof on the plaintiff. The defendant doesn't usually have to prove anything, but need only disprove the plaintiff's evidence.

Courtroom Demeanor: How to Put Your Best Foot Forward

Here are a few tips on how to behave during a courtroom trial, whether you are the plaintiff or the defendant.

- Make sure you attend every day of the trial. If you are absent, the jury might think you don't care, and you could lose your case.
- Make sure you appear on time.
- Remember, you are trying to impress a jury, so it's a good idea to dress appropriately.
- Don't attempt to communicate with your attorney while testimony is being given or when he is addressing the court.
- Don't argue with your attorney in view of the judge or jury.
- Take notes during the proceedings, so that you can discuss them with your attorney later.
- Be polite and act with respect toward the judge, the opposing attorney, and any witnesses. Don't make faces, speak, or otherwise react to the testimony and the evidence.
- When called upon to speak, make sure you are heard.
- Answer all questions truthfully.
- If your attorney objects to a question asked of you, don't answer it until instructed to do so by the judge.
- Don't volunteer any information.

Opening Statements

The trial begins with the attorney for the plaintiff addressing the jury. This opening statement presents the outline of the plaintiff's view of the case and a preview of the proof of his claims. Next, the defendant's attorney makes an opening statement, presenting his view of the case and a preview of his version of the evidence concerning the plaintiff's claims. The defense attorney is permitted to waive his opening statement and wait until the plaintiff's case is completed before addressing the jury.

Presentation of Evidence

After the opening statements, the presentation of evidence begins. That evidence must be legally admissible. What is legally admissible is governed by a complex set of rules known as the rules of evidence, which basically boil down to this: Evidence must be relevant (related to the fact to be proved), competent (admissible under the rules of evidence), and material (directly related to the fact in a way that helps to prove that fact). It is the job of the judge to rule on the admissibility of the evidence. Evidentiary rulings are important because they help lay the basis for the jury verdict, and errors in admitting evidence may provide the basis for an appeal.

The plaintiff is first to present evidence. There are two major classes of evidence: testimony and physical evidence. Testimony is evidence given orally by a witness. Physical evidence encompasses all other forms of evidence, such as documents, photographs, and objects. These classes of evidence are further divided into direct evidence and indirect evidence. Direct evidence immediately establishes the fact to be proved. Indirect evidence establishes facts from which the fact to be proved can be inferred. Circumstantial evidence is a form of indirect evidence; it establishes circumstances from which the fact to be proved can be inferred.

Both sides call witnesses to support their case. Basically, there are two kinds of witnesses: lay and expert. A lay witness is one who does not necessarily have any special skills in a particular field, but has knowledge of relevant facts. An eyewitness who observes an accident is a lay witness.

An expert witness is someone who, by virtue of knowledge, training, education, skill, or experience in a specialized area, has information not generally known by the layman. For instance, in a personal injury case, a physician who treated the injured plaintiff would be considered an expert witness, since he would be testifying about subjects the average juror would not know.

Witnesses may be cross-examined by either side. They may appear either voluntarily or by subpoena, which is an order by the court to appear and testify. If a witness is required to bring anything with him, such as medical or financial records, a special kind of subpoena, called a *subpoena duces tecum* (which freely translated means *bring the goods with you*) is issued. When documents or other evidence are used or introduced by witnesses, or are introduced directly by the attorneys, they are generally referred to as "Exhibit A," "Exhibit B," and so forth.

After the plaintiff's case is completed (rested) the defendant has the right to make a motion, a request to the judge to dismiss the case on the basis that a case has not been made. Since the burden of proof is on the plaintiff, he must attempt to make a prima facie case, a presentation of sufficient evidence that "on first view" supports his claim and a possible verdict in his favor. When the defense makes such a motion to dismiss, it is, in effect, asking the judge to rule that such a prima facie has not been made, and that as a matter of law the jury could not rule in the plaintiff's favor.

If the judge determines that the plaintiff has failed to meet the minimum requirement of proof, he will grant the defendant's motion to dismiss, and the case will be over. If the judge decides that a prima facie case has been made, the motion is denied and the trial continues.

Next up is the defendant's attorney, who will introduce testimony from witnesses and other evidence, the object of which is to disprove the claims presented by the plaintiff. The plaintiff has the right to cross-examine the defendant's witnesses. When this process is completed, that is, when all the defendant's evidence has been introduced, the defendant's attorney will rest his case.

At this point, the plaintiff has the right to bring in rebuttal witnesses, whose purpose is to rebut specific evidence introduced by the defendant. These witnesses, like all others, are subject to cross-examination.

Closing Statements

After both sides rest their case, each is permitted to address the jury in a closing argument or summation. This is a final attempt to influence the jury's verdict by reviewing the evidence and by using the art of persuasion. In most states, the plaintiff argues first, then the defendant argues, and then the plaintiff offers a rebuttal.

The Judge's Charge

After the summations (or sometimes before them), the judge will *charge,* or *instruct,* the jury—that is, he will inform the jury of the law applicable in the case and how to apply the facts in the case to that law to arrive at a verdict. The attorneys for both sides usually propose jury instructions and argue to the judge, without the jury present, about what instructions should be given to the jury before the jury is charged. Errors in jury instructions can result in a case being overturned on appeal and retried, so the attorneys and judge are usually very thorough about the language of jury instructions.

The Verdict

After the members of the jury have received arguments and have been instructed, it is left up to them to reach a verdict in the case. The jury retires to a jury room, where the case is discussed. A foreman is selected to preside over the jury deliberations. At some point the foreman will ask for a vote, which can be secret. In some jurisdictions a unanimous decision is required for a verdict. In others, the decision need not be unanimous. For instance, a five-to-one vote may be a legal verdict on a six-person jury, and a ten-to-two (or sometimes nine-to-three) vote on a twelve-person jury. Usually, the jury in a personal injury case is responsible not only for bringing in a verdict for either the plaintiff or defendant but also, if the verdict is in favor of the plaintiff, for awarding him a specific sum of money to be paid by the defendant as compensation.

If a party to the suit disagrees with the jury's verdict, his attorney can ask the judge to disregard the jury's verdict and instead enter a judgment in that party's favor. This is called a motion for a "judgment notwithstanding the verdict." The motion will be granted only if the judge believes that it is obvious that the jury's verdict was legally incorrect, a very rare occurrence.

STEP FOUR: THE APPEAL

Whether you are the plaintiff or the defendant, if the decision of the jury goes against you, you have the right to appeal to a higher court. However, the appeal must be based primarily on an error in law by the judge in ruling on evidence or in ruling on motions or in jury instructions.

An appeal generally begins with the loser (the appellant) filing a notice of appeal. The appellant must also usually obtain a transcript of the trial and file a brief or memorandum of appeal with the appeals court. This brief or memorandum details the alleged legal errors and the arguments of the appellant justifying reversal on appeal. The appellee then files a brief or memorandum to counter the appellant's claims. The appellant may then file a reply responding to the appellee's arguments, and in some courts the appellee has one final opportunity to answer the reply.

The appellate court reaches its decision either from an examination of papers submitted by the parties or from oral arguments made by both parties, or from both. The appellate court can decide to affirm the lower court's decision, in which case the verdict stands, or it can reverse the lower court's decision, in which case the verdict is overturned. If the verdict is overturned, the case may be sent back for a new trial.

The appeals process is usually a long one, sometimes taking a number of years. For this reason, both parties might be willing to sit down and negotiate a settlement even after the jury's verdict has come in. It may be well worth it for both the plaintiff and the defendant to settle rather than endure an appeal and perhaps another trial. Once again, it should be pointed out that a settlement may be agreed on at any time during the trial, during jury deliberation, or even after the verdict has been announced.

STEP FIVE: COLLECTION OF JUDGMENT

Once the verdict has been reached and the appeal, if there is one, has been resolved, the plaintiff is entitled to collect the award. When there is insurance, the insurance company usually will pay the judgment. But if there is no insurance, legal steps may have to be taken to collect the award.

First, the judgment is filed or recorded in an official place of judgment records, such as the office of the county clerk. The plaintiff is now called the judgment creditor, and the defendant is the judgment debtor. If the judgment debtor refuses to pay, the judgment creditor may, subject to requirements of the jurisdiction, summon the debtor to a proceeding supplementary to judgment, in which the debtor is examined under oath concerning his assets. If the debtor has any assets, they may be taken to pay the judgment. If the debtor still refuses to pay, the creditor can obtain a court-issued execution, which is an order to an officer of the court to seize the debtor's assets, from which the judgment will be paid.

. . .

Litigation can be a difficult, uncertain, expensive, and drawn-out affair. This is probably the major reason why more than 95 percent of all personal injury cases are settled before trial.

Because litigation can be so prolonged, there can be extended periods when nothing is happening, and the client may not hear from his attorney because there is nothing to report. Some clients feel neglected. They become anxious, frustrated, and even angry. However, the client must understand that the process is often slow and cumbersome and that this is not necessarily the fault of the attorney. Nevertheless, if three or four months go by without any word from your attorney, there is nothing wrong with calling to ask if there have been any changes in the status of your case.

CHAPTER FIVE

THE NEGLIGENCE AND

INSURANCE

CONTROVERSIES

THE UNITED STATES is often criticized for being the most litigious country in the world. This may appear to be a rather damning criticism. However, upon further examination, litigation is consistent with our history and culture. After all, America is a democracy, based on the notion of liberty and equality for all. It is logical that we would develop a democratic method to ensure economic compensation for a person who suffers injuries as the result of someone else's wrongdoing. That method is our judicial system. Consequently, when there is damage to property or to one's person—for example due to someone else's negligence—the recourse under our legal system lies in either the threat of or the actual institution of a legal action.

In many personal injury cases, the monetary damages, which are the responsibility of the person who caused the injury, might be well beyond his ability to pay. For this reason, most of us carry the appropriate kind of insurance—a homeowner's liability policy, automobile insurance, or if you are a professional such as an attorney or a doctor, malpractice insurance. In the event of an accident in which you are at fault, your insurance company pays the damages up to your policy limit.

Because there is money to be made in the insurance business, there is a good deal of competition among insurance carriers. In advertising campaigns that appear in all the media, as well as in person-to-person pitches, insurance companies stress the dangers of being without coverage. Of course, we pay insurance premiums for this coverage, and it is a matter of record that rates charged by the insurance carriers for policies of every kind have risen sharply over the years.

Consumers have complained bitterly about these escalating insurance rates and recently many state legislatures have introduced bills that would roll back the cost of premiums. In California, for instance, a proposition aimed at rolling back automobile insurance rates 20 percent was passed a few years ago. Within a year, more than fourteen thousand such bills were brought before other state legislatures in an attempt to control an industry that is virtually without any federal regulation.

One of the strategies used by the insurance industry to fight these rollbacks, as well as to justify rising premiums, is to point to escalating costs and lower profits. One of the industry's favorite scapegoats has been the legal system and, in particular, attorneys. The industry claims that a great number of suits have been encouraged by attorneys. The costs involved in going to court, not to mention some of the high settlements attorneys are able to obtain, have caused the insurance industry's expenses to shoot through the roof. Simply as a defensive measure, so that they can continue to show even a small profit for their shareholders, the companies say, they have been forced to raise their rates. They maintain that if there were fewer suits and fewer huge recoveries, rates wouldn't be nearly as high. In fact, they would probably come down.

On the face of it, there is a certain logic to that argument. But when it is examined more closely, several glaring fallacies become apparent. It's true that of late many insurance companies have faced an economic crisis, but is the "crisis" really due to what they would call frivolous suits brought with little foundation? Or, rather, is it due to a self-inflicted insurance industry profit cycle and to their own poor investments? When interest rates were high, the industry cut prices in order to obtain premium dollars to invest at high interest rates. When interest rates, and thus investment income, dropped, the insurance industry responded by sharply increasing premiums and reducing availability. Articles in The Wall Street Journal and comments by industry leaders themselves confirm this point of view.

In addition a December 2, 1990, article in *The New York Times/The Business World Magazine,* which focused on the problems of the insurance industry today, described the many poor investments insurances companies have made in the last decade or so, including seriously underperforming mortgages and speculation in junk bonds, lower-grade municipal bonds, private placements, and foreign loans.

Furthermore, the argument made by insurance companies makes it appear that millions or billions of dollars are paid in suits brought over minor accidents for no other reason than to harass the insurance carriers and reap an undeserved bonanza for the accident victim and his attorney. This is hardly the case. For years the average citizen did not know that he had the right to avail himself of our judicial system. Only in the recent past have people become more aware of their rights. As a result, more claims have been made. Evidence shows, however, that any increase in claims is minimal and consistent with the growth in population, not litigants running wild.

This may upset many segments of society, the insurance companies and wrongdoers among them. But in reality it is a healthy condition. Every American should be able to avail himself of our legal system, not just those who are rich enough or sophisticated enough to know how the legal system works or to have a family attorney. Besides, those who are victims of an accident caused by the negligence of another deserve to be fairly compensated for the damages incurred.

In fact, our legal system does work and it works quite well.

It discourages people from doing dangerous things. For example, it prevents businesses from putting harmful products into the marketplace, because they know that if they are responsible for harm, they will have to pay for the damages caused by that harm. Our legal system simply enforces that responsibility. Of course, people are worried about being sued if they do something wrong, but is that so bad? Perhaps they should be worried. Perhaps it will cause them to be more careful, more mindful of their behavior and the consequences of their conduct.

There is another fallacy in the arguments made by the insurance companies. Statistics don't show that these companies are necessarily losing money as a result of too many lawsuits. The truth is, although there have been a few large recoveries in lawsuits over product liability and such environmental disasters as the *Exxon Valdez* oil spill in 1989, the number of these cases is actually small. In fact, the average settlement or verdict is twenty thousand dollars or less, and these companies make more money than they pay out simply because the vast majority of people who purchase policies don't file claims. In addition, insurance companies have extremely large reserve funds, earning interest while cases languish in the judicial system. Consequently, there is and always will be a built-in profit margin for insurance companies, so long as they make wise rather than risky investments of their capital.

Another argument sometimes offered by those who criticize our legal system is that it has stifled free enterprise in this country by squelching the production of new products. The argument runs something like this: Because of the stringent safety standards that must be met, due in large part to the potential of huge lawsuits, it has become prohibitively expensive to introduce new products in this country. Furthermore, the argument goes, this is not a problem in other countries, where standards are not quite as high and where there is less risk of paralyzing lawsuits.

But the truth is that the threat of a lawsuit only becomes a problem when products are unsafe and run the risk of bringing harm to people. Good companies making good products carefully don't have a problem. Companies that are afraid of introducing products to the market because they are likely to injure and maim people should be. If they aren't concerned with safety, they shouldn't be in business. As it stands, people, and especially children, are far safer in this country than anywhere else in the world *because* of our legal system, not in spite of it.

The bottom line is that we are unashamedly a capitalistic, entrepreneurial country in which efficiency and competence are rewarded. To create a product that is defective and harmful and will endanger the public at large is not desired or encouraged in our society. It is punishable by law, and in the end, there is no doubt that such diligence might slightly raise the price of both products and services. But certainly, at the very least, from the point of view of the person who would be injured, it is well worth it. Perhaps even more important is that our legal system not only discourages companies from producing a product they know is dangerous, but also provides a strong incentive for everyone to be aware of their behavior and its consequences, and to conform to certain basic standards of care.

Consider the possible alternatives. One suggestion that has been made is to construct a system to deal with all negligence cases, similar to that used in worker's compensation cases (which will be discussed in full in Chapter 13), wherein certain types of injuries are rated as being worth a certain number of dollars, no more, no less. This procedure would do away with most of the civil court system, since there would be no jury serving to evaluate fair compensation for an injury. But the price one gets paid for an injury under such a system would be purely arbitrary. Furthermore, a disturbingly low value is usually placed on an injury in worker's compensation cases, with no leeway for individual circumstances, such as how the injury might affect the victim's future earnings and lifestyle. Besides running the risk of removing some of the incentives for responsible behavior, such a system also ignores the important psychological and emotional factors of receiving compensation for an injury on the basis of the actual effect it has.

Under the present system, the court allows a jury to decide

what an injury is worth, rather than allowing bureaucrats to decide. There might be occasional inequities, but in the end, it is the public, in the form of a jury of one's peers, that decides what does and what does not constitute a valid claim. Otherwise, we would have to appoint someone to decide what is negligent and what isn't, as well as what will fairly compensate a particular injury.

Admittedly, we have an imperfect and often inefficient system, but ultimately there are checks and balances that make it work. For instance, if a jury awards an outrageously large verdict, the defendant may appeal, or the judge hearing the case may exercise his discretion in reducing the verdict or ordering a new trial. This does occur in many of the cases that make headlines.

It has been our experience that the majority of juries do the right thing. They decide what the community standards of conduct are and then return a verdict that appears to be commensurate with the injury and the degree of negligent behavior. In short, while our present legal system may sometimes seem cumbersome and expensive, in the long run it works.

THE NO-FAULT INSURANCE CONTROVERSY

In the early 1970s, in an effort to save time and money for consumers and the courts, several states passed so-called no-fault laws that guaranteed motorists automatic coverage for injuries sustained in automobile accidents. At the same time, some of these statutes, such as those in New Jersey, still allowed motorists to sue for pain and suffering when the medical expenses exceeded a certain amount (in New Jersey, the figure was two hundred dollars).

By enacting no-fault laws, legislatures hoped to lower car insurance premiums by reducing the number of lawsuits and the number of claims, while at the same time reducing the amount that the insurance carriers paid for claims. In turn, this savings was supposed to be passed on to the consumer in the form of reduced premiums. The trade-off was simple. In no-fault states, depending upon the particular jurisdiction, the injured party usually gives up his or her right to sue. This particularly applies to the category of soft-tissue injuries (whiplash, sprains, strains, and so forth).

However, in cases of more serious injuries lawsuits are generally still permitted, although stringent rules governing them are in force. In most no-fault states, for instance, you cannot sue unless you meet the "threshold of injury." This threshold includes dismemberment injuries causing significant limitation of bodily motion and neck and back problems. These injuries must result in the victim's not being able to perform normal duties for a certain period of time (usually, at least ninety days), and appropriate medical proof must be provided. During this ninety-day period, regular medical treatment must be received and you must be out of work, usually for at least two weeks (a doctor's written recommendation is required).

At first, these no-fault laws, most of which differ somewhat from state to state, had the enthusiastic support of consumer groups. After all, the ultimate goal of the plan was to unburden the court system and lower premiums. Unfortunately, it didn't quite work out that way. Now, almost twenty years after the first no-fault laws were enacted, consumer groups are reevaluating their views of the efficacy of these laws. For instance, longtime consumer advocate Ralph Nader has taken a very strong position against no-fault because he believes that the courts are the best place to pursue a remedy, and that no-fault has only harmed consumers, not helped them.

It's true that the number of lawsuits has been reduced in many of those states, but premiums have not gone down. In fact, in no state have the premiums on automobile insurance ever been reduced. No-fault laws have also resulted in a quagmire of bureaucratic red tape. This has not gone unnoticed by consumer groups or legislators and, as a result, changes seem likely.

For instance, in 1988 the State of California (not a no-fault state) passed an initiative that required a 20 percent reduction in automobile insurance rates (as of today, this decision is still being fought in the courts by the insurance industry). Other states, such as New Jersey, are actively reassessing their no-fault laws with the notion of either revoking them altogether or appreciably restructuring them. No new state has adopted no-fault insurance for years and, in fact, several states have abolished their no-fault systems to return to the traditional fault-based system.

MAKING SENSE OUT OF NONSENSE: HOW TO PURCHASE AN INSURANCE POLICY

One of the most difficult and confusing tasks faced by consumers as well as personal injury attorneys today is dealing with insurance policies. To begin with, many of these policies are written so that it is almost impossible for the average person to read and understand them. In addition, insurance companies seem to be putting every condition and restriction they can into their policies so that they won't have to pay off on a claim. Nevertheless, they must give some kind of basic coverage to justify the cost of their premiums.

The majority of people purchase their insurance policies through an agent. These policies are usually very detailed and complicated. As a result, the average consumer has only a vague notion of what the policy actually covers. In many instances, it isn't until the consumer has an accident or makes a claim that he finds out what the policy actually covers. For instance, some homeowner's policies have what are called exclusionary clauses, which preclude certain members of the family who reside in the household from collecting on the policy. The aim of such clauses is theoretically to stop family members from arranging phony accidents and then making fraudulent claims for them. But they also prevent payment for some accidents caused by real negligence.

Exclusionary clauses are just one example of the kinds of restrictive clauses contained in a policy that you might not be aware of until it's too late. For this reason, it's a good idea to read any policy you purchase very carefully. If you don't understand something, ask about it. And if you don't get a satisfactory answer, ask again. If possible, try to get what's called an easy read policy, that is, one that is written in terms the layman can understand. If the policy is a complicated one, it might be worthwhile to show it to an attorney.

You may purchase your insurance either directly from the individual company or through an independent agent, who might represent several companies. One question we are often asked is, Should I use an agent or should I go directly to the insurance carrier? There's no simple answer, although it is a good idea to shop around, since independent agents might handle only a limited number of insurance companies and the companies themselves, of course, will sell only their own policies. The advantage of dealing with an independent agent is that, presumably, you have someone familiar to go to when you have a problem.

Sometimes, an insurance agent may be held responsible for failing to sell you appropriate insurance. For instance, not long ago a client came to us with a case that concerned his insurance coverage. He owned an automobile repair shop and had recently purchased an insurance policy to cover his tool shed. One morning he arrived at work to find that the shed had been broken into and all his tools, which were valued at several thousand dollars, had been stolen. Believing that he was covered by his policy, he called his agent and reported the theft, only to be informed that the tools were not covered. Distraught, he came to us to see if anything could be done.

It could. After investigating the case our attorney found that the client had specifically asked for and sincerely believed that he had obtained theft insurance covering the contents of the shed. Unfortunately, the agent had simply neglected to include such coverage in the policy. Consequently, the agent was determined to have been negligent and our client was able to recover the value of the tools.

However, there was a good chance our client could have recovered even if he hadn't specifically asked for theft coverage, so long as it could be shown that, under normal circumstances, the agent should have included this kind of coverage as a matter of course. If the matter came to trial, the plaintiff would have to prove the case by calling expert witnesses in the field who would testify that the coverage should have been offered.

As a general rule, it is wise to carry an adequate amount of insurance. If there's any question concerning the matter of adequate coverage, it's best to consult an attorney.

CHAPTER SIX

AUTOMOBILE INSURANCE

As THE NUMBER of automobiles on the road has increased dramatically over the past forty years, so has the number of automobile accidents. And with the increase of accidents, legislators began to look for ways to compensate people for their losses and injuries. As a result, a number of states have enacted laws that require that all automobiles driven within that state be insured. If they are not, the owner may be fined and may have his driver's license and automobile registration suspended.

Automobile insurance coverage may be divided into three categories: collision, liability, and comprehensive coverage.

COLLISION INSURANCE

Surprisingly, we have found that many clients, even if they are severely injured in an accident, are at first more concerned about who is responsible for repairing their car. Under a collision insurance policy, the owner of the vehicle is entitled to reimbursement for any damage to that vehicle that comes as the result of a collision with another object, which would include another vehicle, a building, an abutment, or a tree.

In order to reduce the premiums for this coverage, many companies include deductibles, usually in the amount of fifty or one hundred dollars, in their policies. Consequently, if the damage is less than the amount of the deductible, the policyholder must pay for the damage himself. If the loss is greater than the deductible amount, the insurance company will pay the amount of the damage minus the deductible. For instance, suppose that you hit a mailbox coming out of your driveway and the damage to your car is $150. The deductible in your policy is $100. If you choose to make a claim you would be responsible for paying the first $100 and your insurance company would pay the remaining $50. In such cases, however, you might choose not to make a claim for such a small amount, since your premium might increase.

To take another example, suppose that you were in an accident, the other driver was at fault, and your car was seriously damaged, but you were not injured. You need the car, so you have to have it repaired as soon as possible. But if the other driver's insurance carrier pays for the repairs, it will send an adjuster to evaluate the damage and that might mean you won't have your car for several weeks, perhaps even longer. On the other hand, under your collision policy, you can ask your own insurance carrier to pay for the repairs (minus the deductible), and then it will collect the money from the other driver's carrier and perhaps even have your deductible reimbursed.

LIABILITY INSURANCE

Liability insurance covers the owner of a specific motor vehicle for any liability that comes as a result of the negligent operation of that vehicle. These policies are usually renewable each year. They contain a liability limit and a promise by the insurance carrier to defend any lawsuit brought against the holder of the policy for any claims that relate to the operation of that vehicle. There are, of course, several stipulations included in the average contract, such as giving the company timely notice of any accident, as well as a promise by the policyholder to cooperate, appear, and testify in any lawsuit that comes as a result of the accident.

Some policies allow the holder the option of carrying what

is referred to as "medical payments" (or "med-pay") coverage. This option will add a little to the cost of your policy, but because of the benefits if offers, it's usually well worth it. Generally, med-pay reimburses you and your passengers for injuries occuring in your car regardless of whose fault the accident was, up to a certain total amount for medical expenses incurred within a certain period (often a year) after the accident.

If you are a passenger in an automobile involved in an accident, find out if the insurance policy of your driver as well as the other driver includes a med-pay provision. The advantage of med-pay is that it usually reimburses 100 percent of medical expenses and, if you collect for your injuries from other sources, you usually don't have to repay the med-pay carrier. For instance, if you have a separate health-care policy, you will usually receive those benefits in addition to your med-pay benefits. However, there is a recent trend for health insurance carriers to try to get money back from automatic liability insurers.

NO-FAULT INSURANCE

As mentioned in the previous chapter, many states have now adopted some form of no-fault insurance. Under this system, which was developed in Massachusetts some twenty years ago, any driver, passenger, or pedestrian who is injured in an automobile accident will automatically get his or her medical expenses and lost wages paid by the insurance company involved, regardless of who was at fault.

The premise of no-fault is that the owner of the vehicle must buy a minimum amount of no-fault insurance in order to be allowed to drive that vehicle. In return, if you are injured in an accident involving that vehicle, you will be compensated by your own insurance carrier regardless of who was at fault. For instance, suppose that you ran into another car and you were at fault. No-fault insurance would cover the damages to your automobile as well as the medical bills and the wages you lose. However, in some states there are exceptions that may prevent you from collecting. If you, the driver of the vehicle, were under the influence of alcohol at the time of the accident, for example, you probably will not be compensated by your own carrier.

In many jurisdictions, under no-fault laws, you are prohibited from suing the other driver unless you can either show that your economic losses exceed a certain predetermined level or show that your injuries included some specific serious conditions. In other jurisdictions, you are allowed to sue at any time but, if you collect from the defendant, you must reimburse your no-fault insurer for any payments they have made.

To give you a better idea of what a no-fault insurance law covers, here are some of the features of the New York State law.

1. No-fault coverage includes payment for all doctor bills, for which there are rate schedules that limit the amount a doctor can charge.
2. All hospital bills are covered, although they are also subject to rate limitations.
3. You may receive up to twenty-five dollars a day for other necessary expenses, which would include: a) someone to care for you, if such care is necessary. For you to receive compensation for this care a statement must be provided from the attending physician authorizing these services; b) reimbursement for transportation expenses that come as a result of traveling to and from medical treatment (it's a good idea to keep comprehensive records of such travel).
4. Medical needs, including medication, prescriptions, crutches, bandages, hospital beds, and wheelchairs, are covered. Again, these items must be prescribed by your attending physician.
5. If you are unable to work as a result of the injuries sustained in the accident, the insurance company will pay 80 percent of your gross regular wages. However, there are certain deductibles as well as maximums, which are dependent upon coverage. These benefits will not begin to be paid until the insurance company receives a form from your physician in which he indicates that you are unable

to work due to injuries suffered in the accident. It is also necessary for your employer to indicate the amount of your gross earnings, dates you lost time from work, the normal number of hours and days worked each week, and so forth.

Under New York's no-fault law, if you are seriously injured, you may still recover for your pain and suffering if you sue. However, in order to qualify to sue, you must have sustained a "serious injury," which is defined by the law as being one of the following types:

- Death.
- Dismemberment.
- Significant disfigurement.
- A fracture.
- Significant loss of the use of a body organ, member, function, or system.
- Permanent limitation of use of a body organ or member that came as a consequence of the injury.
- Medically determined injury or impairment of a nonpermanent nature that prevents the injured party from performing substantially all the material acts that constitute that party's usual and customary daily activities for not less than 90 days during the 180 days immediately following the occurrence of the injury or impairment.

COMPREHENSIVE INSURANCE

Under a comprehensive insurance policy the insured is covered against damage to the vehicle that comes as the result of such things as theft, fire, vandalism, falling objects, acts of nature (earthquake, hurricane, and so forth), and explosion. As in the case of collision insurance, these policies often include a deductible.

UNDERINSURED AND UNINSURED POLICIES

What do you do if you're in an accident in a state with fault-based insurance and the person at fault doesn't have insurance? Are you out of luck? Not necessarily. You may have what is called uninsured motorist coverage written into your policy (some states even require this coverage). Having this coverage means that if you're injured by a negligent driver who has no insurance at all, your own insurance company will pay what his insurance would have paid if he had some. Underinsured motorage coverage is insurance that pays you when the negligent driver's policy is not large enough to pay for all the damages. Uninsured or underinsured motorist insurance is usually rather inexpensive and, in our opinion, it's absolutely necessary. In fact, with a large percentage of drivers being uninsured, this may turn out to be the most useful coverage you purchase.

WHO IS COVERED UNDER YOUR INSURANCE POLICY?

The policy itself usually dictates who will be covered under your insurance policy. For that reason, it's absolutely imperative that you read your policy closely. You, the owner, are covered, and the following *may,* depending on how your individual policy is written, also be included in your coverage:

- Anyone using your car with your permission.
- Anyone living within your household.
- Certain relatives.
- Employees (depending upon whether they are using your vehicle as part of their work).

Again, those covered depend upon the way the individual policy is written. So don't take anything for granted.

Some states have what are called "permissive use" statutes, which make the owner of a vehicle liable for injuries caused by the carelessness of anyone driving the car with that owner's permission. In other states, the owner is not liable unless he is personally guilty of a negligent act, such as failing to maintain the vehicle in proper working condition. So, for instance, if you know that your brakes have a tendency to stick and you lend your car to a friend and that friend has an accident because the brakes didn't work, you may be liable for damages arising from that accident.

But whether states do or do not have "permissive use" statutes, you are, in any state, liable for injuries if you loan your car to someone you know is an unsafe driver. For example, suppose that you loan your car to a friend who you know has been in several traffic accidents and has a history of getting speeding tickets. If that friend is in an accident in your car, you may be liable for any damages that ensue from that accident.

Insofar as family is concerned, some states follow what is known as the "family purpose doctrine," which holds the owner of a car liable for injuries that come as a result of a spouse or a child driving that car on a family errand. For instance, if you send your teenage son to the store to pick up a carton of milk and he gets into an accident, you may be held liable for the damages resulting from that accident. In those states that have "permissive use" statutes, you would be held liable for damages arising from a family member's accident whether or not he was on a family errand.

If someone steals your car and then gets into an accident, it is also possible that you may be held liable for the damages. If the car was locked with no keys inside and someone breaks in and steals it, you are not liable. However, if the car was unlocked with the key inside and the motor running, you would be held liable, since the argument could be made that by your careless action you were "inviting" someone to steal your car.

WHAT TO DO IF YOU ARE IN AN ACCIDENT

If you're involved in an automobile accident, certainly you're under a good deal of pressure. Nevertheless, you should have the presence of mind to take several simple steps. Even if you can follow only some of them, it may save you a good deal of trouble down the line.

1. If someone is injured in an accident or if there is damage beyond a small dent or scratch (the dollar amount of damage would usually have to exceed one hundred or two hundred dollars), report the accident to the police. If the police don't arrive at the scene, make sure you go to the police station and make a report. If someone is injured, or if there is serious damage, and you fail to make a report, you may face criminal charges, even if you weren't the one who caused the accident. Most insurance carriers require a police report before they will pay a claim.

2. Remain at the scene of the accident until the police arrive and make sure that the other party does, too (within reason).

3. Exchange the following information with the driver of the other car: name; address; telephone number; license number and license plate number; year and make of the car; name, address, and telephone number of the insurance company and agent. If the driver of the car is not the actual owner of the car, get the owner's name, address, and telephone number. Ask to see a picture ID and a copy of the registration.

4. Get the names and addresses of any possible witnesses. Jot down the license plate numbers of any possible witnesses.

5. Don't talk about the accident and, especially, don't admit any fault, since any statement conceding fault on your part may be used against you later. And often, in the confusion of the

moment, you can't really be certain who was actually at fault, so it's best to say nothing.

6. When the police arrive, tell them what happened in the accident. If you think the other party did something wrong, tell the police right away. Get the names and badge numbers of police officers who arrive on the scene, as well as the police station where their report will be filed and, if available, the report number.

7. If it's feasible, make either written or mental notes of the relevant details of the accident, such as road and weather conditions. If at all possible, have photographs taken of both cars at the scene of the accident from several angles. Look around to see if there are any unusual circumstances, such as nonworking traffic lights or hidden stop signs.

8. If there is only property damage, it's usually not necessary to contact an attorney, so call your insurance company as soon as possible.

9. If you have suffered an injury, after you've seen a doctor, it's a good idea to call an attorney even before you call your insurance company, for several reasons. First, in the case of personal injury, someone should monitor your insurance company to make sure that you're being treated fairly. Second, an attorney specializing in personal injury law is best able to evaluate what needs to be done about your accident. Most people simply don't know what to do to document their claim and protect their rights. A good attorney does. A skilled attorney will also be able to tell you how you should proceed. The attorney will take care of such details as getting the police report, investigating the

accident, talking to witnesses, and seeing to it that you are able to get adequate medical treatment. You can then concentrate on your medical treatment and recovery.

10. Get medical attention. Obviously, if you are very seriously injured, this is always the first thing you must do. Even if you don't believe you're seriously injured, it's still a good idea to be examined in an emergency room, since many serious injuries do not become immediately apparent to the injured person. For instance, you may feel fine right after the accident, but several days later you may experience headaches and blurred vision which could be the result of serious head or neck injuries.

11. Obtain a copy of the police report (if you have an attorney, he will take care of this for you). This report, which contains a detailed account of the accident, may be your single most important document. It should take from a week to ten days to obtain the report (in some jurisdictions, it might even take longer), for which you will have to pay a small fee. Once you receive the report, read it and, if you find any errors in it, try to get them corrected. You may do this by sending a certified letter, return receipt requested, to the department that prepared the report. Be sure to identify the report, usually by number.

12. If necessary, get regular treatment for your injuries, and be sure to follow the doctor's instructions.

13. Contact the Department of Motor Vehicles to find out whether you are required to file a report of the accident. Speak with your attorney.

.   .   .

14. Keep a detailed diary of your injuries, including any medical treatment and expenses incurred as a result of the accident. Your diary should include the following, making sure that you also note the dates:

- A daily record of your symptoms and your healing progress, indicating the length of time it takes for all your injuries to heal, as well as the kinds of limitations you experience in your everyday life.
- Dates of all stays at the hospital, as well as outpatient visits.
- Your patient identification card number.
- All visits by nurses and physical therapists.
- All other contacts with medical personnel.
- All medical treatments received.
- All prescribed medications.
- All physicians' names.
- All medical bills.
- Mileage to and from treatment, as well as car rental cost, if this was necessary.
- Damage to your clothing or other personal property as a result of the accident.
- Lost work time due to your injury (be precise as to dates).
- Lost earnings.

15. Obtain a disability slip from your doctor. Make sure it's a written rather than an oral statement.

These are the things you ought to do if you're involved in an accident, but there are also some things you shouldn't do. These include:

- Do not discuss the issue of fault, except with your attorney. This will be decided at a later time.
- Don't reveal the amount of your insurance coverage.

- Don't get into an argument with anyone.
- Don't sign any statements or talk to anyone except your attorney or a representative of your insurance company (but only after consulting with your attorney).
- Don't speak to the insurance company. If you are contacted by an insurance adjuster representing the other party's insurance carrier, he or she may ask you for a statement. Don't give it. The adjuster may also ask to tape the conversation with you. Don't do it. The adjuster may try to settle the case with a promise of quick money. Don't accept it. Instead, refer the adjuster to your attorney. Once you do this, the adjuster is ethically prohibited from dealing with you directly.

PART TWO

HOW TO HELP

YOURSELF:

CASE STUDIES IN

PERSONAL INJURY

CHAPTER SEVEN

MOTOR VEHICLE

ACCIDENTS

EVERY MOTOR VEHICLE accident is slightly different—in time, place, circumstance, and the extent of injury, for example. But a number of general principles and procedure can be illustrated by individual cases.

PEDESTRIAN CASES

Look Who's Sleeping in My Bed

Early one January morning one of our attorneys in California received a call from someone in a local hospital. Introducing himself as Guy, he asked the attorney to come down and help him. When the attorney asked what the problem was, Guy replied rather vaguely that he wasn't quite sure.

When the attorney arrived at the hospital he found Guy lying in a bed, his leg broken in three places and his wrist fractured. Naturally, the attorney asked what happened.

"I don't really know," Guy replied.

"Just tell me what you do know," the attorney said.

"Well, it was New Year's Eve. I'd been out celebrating a

little. I was walking down the street, on my way to another party, and that's the last thing I remember."

Since Guy couldn't remember much beyond that, the attorney took the necessary steps to obtain the police report, which he hoped would be more helpful. Unfortunately, it wasn't. The report was rather garbled, not shedding much more light on what had happened to Guy. Still baffled, the attorney called the investigating police officer, informed him that he was representing Guy, and pressed him for more information.

This is what the police officer had been able to piece together: It was early morning, New Year's Day, and Guy had been doing some serious celebrating. As soon as he got to the hospital, his blood was tested for alcohol content and it came up 0.23, more than twice the amount for which you are presumed to be legally drunk. He was walking down the sidewalk, and apparently someone even drunker than Guy was driving down the street in an El Camino open-bed pickup truck with a mattress in the back. The truck jumped the curb and hit Guy, who sailed up into the air and landed in the back of the truck, right on the mattress. Evidently, the driver was so drunk that he didn't even realize he had hit anyone, so he simply continued his twenty-mile drive back home.

Once he arrived there and started getting out of his truck, he heard noise, moaning sounds, coming from behind him somewhere. So he went to the back of the truck and was shocked to find a stranger lying on the mattress, bleeding and moaning in pain. Still not realizing what had happened, the driver, incensed, called the police to complain.

Minutes later the police arrived, along with an ambulance. The police officer then examined the truck and found that the front grill was crushed. He rang the doorbell and the driver of the El Camino answered. "Are you the one who called?" the police officer asked.

The man answered, "Yes," and he was immediately arrested. A short while later, the driver was tested, and his blood alcohol level turned out to be an astounding 0.3, just about three times the legal limit denoting drunkenness.

With this information in hand, the accident victim's attorney called the driver's insurance adjuster, told him this incredible tale, and after the adjuster confirmed the details, the insurance carrier agreed to issue a check for the policy limit. Because of the decidedly odd nature of this accident, the settlement went rather smoothly. But besides being amusingly bizarre, this was a fascinating case because it raised an interesting issue in terms of comparative negligence. After all, both Guy and the driver of the El Camino were legally drunk. Why was the adjuster so quick to settle? Why didn't he claim that because Guy was drunk he should be held to some level of comparative negligence?

The answer was simple. No matter how drunk Guy was, he was still walking on the sidewalk where he had every right to be and his drunken condition had absolutely nothing to do with the accident. However, if Guy had been walking in the street, weaving back and forth, instead of on the sidewalk, a jury could easily have found that there was also negligence on his part, and this would have limited his recovery.

But even had this negative factor existed, there might have been another factor that would have negated any claim of comparative negligence. In many states, if you are grossly negligent, as was the driver of the El Camino, you cannot turn around and claim that the victim of the accident was comparatively negligent. For instance, suppose that you are intoxicated (under the legal definition) and driving ninety miles an hour in a school zone when a car fails to stop completely at a stop sign, and you hit that vehicle. Under normal circumstances you might be able to claim that the driver of that car was comparatively negligent because he should have come to a full stop and seen you coming. But because you were drunk and going ninety miles an hour, you would be considered grossly negligent and would not be permitted to avail yourself of a comparative negligence defense.

Before we discuss any other individual cases involving injuries to pedestrians, we should explain that there are a couple of general principles that apply. For one thing, most states have enacted laws that declare that the driver of a vehicle must yield the right of way to a pedestrian. For another, under most circumstances if you, as a pedestrian, are hit by a car, you are able to collect only from the driver's insurance company. One exception to this would occur in a product liability case. For instance, suppose that you were walking down the sidewalk and suddenly a car went out of control due to a defective steering mechanism, jumped the curb, and hit you. You could make a claim against the driver, but suppose that you were seriously injured and the driver had limited insurance. You would also have a claim against the manufacturer of the defective automobile on the basis of product liability.

Look Both Ways Before Crossing

One of our attorneys in California recently represented a young woman whose leg was run over by a tractor trailer. The driver was stopped at a light at an intersection and a pedestrian crossed in front of him. After the pedestrian crossed, the light changed and the driver started to make a right-hand turn. Halfway through the turn, he looked and saw that a young woman was crossing the intersection. He was unable to stop in time and the trailer he was towing ran over the young woman's leg, breaking it in two places.

The attorney representing the driver's insurance company alleged that the young woman was comparatively negligent because she stepped off the curb without paying attention to the Walk–Don't Walk sign. The insurance company refused to settle so the case went to trial. Our attorney argued that even though the light had turned green for the driver, it was still well within the duty of care for him to look out for any pedestrian who had started to cross before the light actually changed.

The jury, taking into consideration the argument of the defendant, brought in a verdict in favor of the plaintiff in the amount of sixty thousand dollars, which was reduced by 20 percent for the young woman's comparative negligence. In other words, the jury awarded the young woman forty eight thousand dollars, because they felt that the driver did, in fact, have the duty to be on the alert for pedestrians regardless of whether he had the light, and that the young woman's comparative negligence only amounted to 20 percent of the cause of the accident.

Comparative negligence can be a tricky thing. It's almost always used by the defendant's attorney in an attempt to lower liability. Yet there is no hard-and-fast rule about how it is applied. That is completely up to the individual jury. Sometimes it is considered as a factor in the settlement, sometimes not. For instance, one of our attorneys in California represented a man who, while driving his car, had his elbow sticking out of the window. A truck carrying a load of bricks passed by and, as it did, a brick dropped off the truck and hit our client's arm, breaking his elbow. The insurance adjuster claimed that our client was comparatively negligent because his arm was out the window. Eventually, the case was settled, primarily because we were able to convince the adjuster that no jury in California, which would more than likely be made up heavily if not exclusively of drivers, was going to consider having your elbow out of the window as being comparatively negligent.

Cross at the Green, Not In Between

Often, municipalities move crosswalks to accommodate changes in traffic flows. In this particular case, the white lines that denoted a cross-walk had been tarred over in an attempt to obliterate them, while the crosswalk was moved a block away. The township also put up a sign declaring "This is no longer a crosswalk." However, over a period of time, the tar began to wear away, the white lines became visible again, and the sign that had been put up to warn pedestrians fell down. As a result, it now took on the appearance of a crosswalk again.

Our client, who was unfamiliar with the area, reached this

point of the street and, thinking that he had the protection of a pedestrian crosswalk, began to cross. Less than halfway across the street, he was hit by a car and several bones were broken. We brought an action against the township (suits against governments will be explained in detail in Chapter 12) for failure to maintain what was, in effect, a noncrosswalk. We won the case, and our client received a verdict for thirty thousand dollars.

There are various other kinds of road crossing cases, as well. Often, they occur in rural areas where there are no crosswalks. We had one case in which our client was crossing at an intersection that didn't have a crosswalk. One car stopped for him but another car, going in the same direction but moving in another lane, didn't stop and, as a result, it struck him.

We felt we had a strong case because this was an area where the pedestrian had little choice but to cross at that spot, even though there wasn't actually a crosswalk there. Making our case even stronger was the fact that one car had stopped to let him cross. We believed that since this car had stopped, the driver of the other car should have seen this and taken extra care. Using this argument, our attorney was able to convince the defendant's insurance company to settle.

Back in Time

George was a mentally impaired forty-two-year-old man who was under the guardianship of his sister. His impairment, which left him with the mental capacity of a young child, came as the result of an injury he had received in the Vietnam War. Every day, at approximately the same time, he got up, dressed himself, and walked the same route to the Veterans Administration Hall where he had coffee and doughnuts. Although George was mentally impaired, he did know the route well and each day, on his way to the hall, he would cross the street at a place where there was a crosswalk, but no stop sign.

Then one day, George arrived at the crosswalk and began crossing the street, whereupon he was hit by a truck. He suffered various facial injuries as well as a broken hip. The driver of the truck, shaken by the accident, said that George had simply stepped off the curb in front of him. He said that he tried to swerve and avoid him, but couldn't.

George's sister visited one of our offices and asked us to represent him in an action against the driver's insurance company. In arguing the case, our attorney claimed that since George did not have the mental capacity of an average person of his age, he should be held to the same standard of care as a person the same mental and emotional age that he was, that is, the standard of a child of about seven or eight. Rather than litigate and have to deal with this argument in front of a jury, the insurance company chose to settle.

If this case hadn't been settled, it would have been left up to the jury to decide whether the standard of care expected of George should have been, due to his mental impairment, only that expected of someone of the same mental capacity. Furthermore, it would have been left up to the jury to decide what that age would have been. Obviously, the insurance company felt it was in its best interests to settle, rather than leave it up to a jury that might come in with a verdict in favor of George.

By the same token, George's attorney obviously felt that it was in his client's best interests to settle quickly, since litigation might take several years. Weighing the time factor against the immediate settlement, the attorney advised George's family that the extra money he might get from a jury trial would probably not justify the anxiety and pressure of a prolonged legal battle.

Hot Time, Summer in the City

It was summertime and it was hot. To get some relief from the heat, a bunch of kids took part in a time-honored tradition by turning on a fire hydrant and letting themselves get sprayed. One of the other things they did to amuse themselves was to direct the spray on cars as they passed by. Sally drove by and, like every other car that came through the spray, her car was squirted on the windshield to such an extent that her vision was obscured. However, she continued moving forward and, in doing so, she hit Dennis, a nine-year-old boy who was playing in the street. Apparently unaware that she had hit anyone, Sally continued driving away. One teenager who had witnessed the accident chased her and finally caught up with her a few blocks away. Fortunately, Dennis sustained relatively minor injuries, including a separated shoulder and several cuts and bruises that required medical attention. An attorney from one of our offices represented Dennis.

The argument presented by Sally's insurance company was twofold. First, it claimed that there had been a lack of parental supervision in allowing the children to play in the street. Second, it argued that due to the spray of water on Sally's windshield, she couldn't see anything in front of her.

To counter those arguments, our attorney maintained that the children weren't doing anything inherently dangerous or out of the ordinary under the circumstances (it was, in fact, a common occurrence for the police department to open these hydrants for the children to play under); and that if Sally really couldn't see anything due to the water on her windshield, she should have stopped the car until she could see. Evidently, these arguments were persuasive, since the insurance company decided to avoid litigation and, instead, settled the case for fifteen thousand dollars.

ACCIDENTS INVOLVING RELATIVES

Would the Real Driver Please Stand Up

A married couple, Elliot and Gail, were taking a car trip from their home in Los Angeles up the coast to San Francisco. He was driving the first leg of the trip. After a couple of hours they decided to stop and have breakfast at a roadside diner. After breakfast, Gail took the wheel. The next thing anyone remembered was that the vehicle had rolled over and Gail, dazed and disoriented, was wandering alongside the highway. The police were called and, when they questioned Gail, they found that she could not remember anything. Elliot was pulled from the wreck and taken to a hospital, where, suffering from massive injuries, he lay in a coma.

The biggest question was who was driving at the time of the accident? Elliot's keys were in the ignition, and Gail remembered driving when they left the diner. However, she didn't remember if she was still driving when the accident, to which there were no witnesses, occurred, and Elliot could shed no light since he remained in a deep coma. The accident had occurred several hours after their breakfast stop and there was a good chance that in between the time they stopped for breakfast and the time they had the accident, they had pulled into a rest stop to use the bathrooms. If they had done that, they might have switched drivers again. But since Gail had no memory of having done that and Elliot was locked in a coma, no one could be sure.

The question of who was driving was important because if Elliot was the driver Gail might have had a claim against him for negligence. But if Gail was driving, he might have had a claim against her for negligence. Since his injuries were far more serious, it would certainly be more advantageous for him to be able to sue her rather than vice versa.

As we mentioned before, however, some insurance policies have an exclusionary clause, which prohibits either spouse from suing the other for negligence. In some states (New York is one of them), there is a rule called spousal immunity, which prohibits one spouse from suing another. Otherwise, in a majority of states, one spouse may sue another (remember, you're really seeking a settlement from an insurance company, not from the person you're suing) for ordinary negligence; while other states allow lawsuits only for injuries resulting from intentional wrongful acts, such as assault.

Gail retained an attorney from one of our offices to represent her. After reading the insurance policy, the attorney ascertained that there was no exclusionary clause, which meant that the spouses could sue each other. But in litigating the suit, the real problem would have come in trying to persuade a jury who was actually driving at the time of the accident. In the end, after some serious soul searching, Gail decided not to pursue the case because she was not psychologically prepared to go through the trauma of what could have been a prolonged legal action. Instead, the couple simply settled on the medical coverage available to them.

In some cases in which two spouses are involved, the litigation may involve what is called a loss of consortium claim; that is, a claim made by one spouse that he or she has, as a result of the accident, lost the love, sexual enjoyment, help, and companionship of the spouse who was injured. However, there are some problems with this kind of claim. In the first place, juries are loath to accept loss of consortium claims. In our experience, they only prove fruitful when there have been catastrophic injuries. Additionally, even when they are accepted by juries, they are rarely worth very much money. Balanced against this is the fact that these claims sometimes open up very private and potentially embarrassing personal areas dealing with sexual intimacy. Given all this, it's sometimes wise to avoid this claim.

Taking Your Mom to Court

In another case, handled by an attorney in one of our New Jersey offices, the client was a nine-year-old boy named David, who was a passenger in a car that his mother was driving. The mother had been drinking and she ran a stoplight. As a result, the car was struck by another car coming across the intersection and David suffered several broken ribs and a broken jaw. One of the options open to David was to sue his mother for negligence.

Years ago, a minor could not sue his parents for injuries that were the result of either negligence or intentional behavior. Today, however, in most states a minor is allowed to sue a parent if that child has suffered damage as the result of that parent's negligent behavior. This is an important change, because if a lawsuit is not permitted, it is then up to the parent to pay for all the child's medical expenses out of pocket. However, if a lawsuit against a parent is allowed, the parent's liability insurance company is liable for these expenses, if there is not a valid "resident relative" exclusion.

A minor cannot bring a lawsuit on his own. A *guardian ad litem* (literally, "guardian for the suit") must be appointed by the court and it is this guardian who will bring the action on behalf of the child. Under most circumstances, the guardian will be either the parent not being sued or a legal guardian named by the court. If this kind of case does make it to the litigation stage, it can sometimes prove difficult for the child plaintiff, because jury members are apt to be somewhat unsympathetic. They might think, "How awful, suing your mother." What the jury often doesn't realize is that the child is really seeking compensation from an insurance company, not the parent. But this obstacle can be surmounted if the child has a competent attorney.

PASSENGERS

In most states, if you, as a driver, are guilty of negligence, you are generally held liable for any injury sustained by any passenger in your vehicle. In some states there are exceptions, such as being prohibited from suing a spouse for negligence, or prohibiting a child from suing a parent. Furthermore, in some states a "social" passenger, that is, one who has not paid for the ride, may not sue the driver even if injuries resulted from that driver's "ordinary" negligence (otherwise defined as simple carelessness). However, if the accident was the result of gross negligence, such as extreme speeding or driving under the influence of alcohol, the passenger is permitted to sue.

In the case of alcohol, some states have ruled that by getting into the vehicle with an intoxicated person, the passenger has assumed the risk that an accident might occur and thereby is precluded from suing. For instance, suppose that you were at a bar with a buddy. He was pretty drunk, but when he offered you a ride home you accepted. You got into an accident and you were injured. Are you comparatively negligent simply by virtue of the fact that you got into the car with him when you knew he was drunk? In those states where such a suit is permitted, it would be up to a jury to decide.

Generally speaking, if you are a passenger in a vehicle that is involved in an accident and you are injured, there are two parties from whom you can seek damages: a) the driver of the vehicle in which you were riding, if he was negligent, or b) the driver of the other car, if he was the cause of the accident. If the other driver is uninsured, you may try to collect from your own or your driver's uninsured motorist insurance carrier.

If you are a passenger in a car involved in an accident, it's often best to retain an attorney other than the one representing the driver of the car in which you were a passenger, even if you don't think that driver did anything wrong. Otherwise, you run the risk of a conflict of interest developing for the attorney, which may be to the detriment of your case.

Pigs Get Fat, Hogs Get Slaughtered

Al, a thirty-seven-year-old plumber, was a passenger in a car driven by his friend Carl. They were only going from Carl's house to the store and back, so they neglected to fasten their seatbelts, although they were in a jurisdiction that mandated by law that seatbelts be worn. They were driving along when they were hit by another car that had run a stop sign. Al was thrown from the car and landed on a fence, which caused his arm to be ripped from its socket. He was right-handed and the injury resulted in the loss of his left arm.

One of our attorneys represented Carl, whose injuries were relatively minor. Eventually, Carl was offered a $10,000 settlement, which he accepted. However, the $400,000 settlement

offered to Al by the insurance company was deemed unacceptable by him and his attorney, so the case went to trial. According to our attorney, who monitored the case, since his client was
called as a witness at Al's trial, the trial occurred in a notoriously conservative jurisdiction. Consequently, the jury came
back with a verdict that set damages at $750,000. If they had
stopped there, that would have been fine with Al. But they did
not. After listening to the testimony of an expert witness who
stated that Al would not have been injured at all if he had worn
a seatbelt in compliance with the law, the jury found that Al
had been comparatively negligent. And by what percentage did
this jury in a notoriously conservative jurisdiction lower the
award? Would you believe 100 percent? That is right. Al wound
up with absolutely nothing.

Of course, in another jurisdiction the verdict might have been
much different. For instance, some juries might totally disregard the fact that Al wasn't wearing a seatbelt. Or, although
they might have found him comparatively negligent for not
wearing one, they might have reduced the award by only 5
percent. There is no hard-and-fast rule. Juries are made up of
individuals and there is no sure way of predicting how they are
going to decide in any given case.

A word here about seatbelts. Many jurisdictions have now
enacted mandatory seatbelt laws for drivers and front-seat passengers. In some jurisdictions, this even extends to the passengers in the back seat of the vehicle. And, as you can see from
the above case, by violating these laws you leave yourself vulnerable to the charge of comparative negligence. Take the case
of a passenger who fails to fasten his seatbelt. There is an
accident. He hits the windshield and sustains serious facial
injuries. Experts for the defense testify that these injuries could
have been prevented, or at the very least partially mitigated, if
he had been wearing a seatbelt. The jury agrees and reduces the
verdict accordingly. Again, it is up to their discretion. At the
very least, even if the case never goes to trial, the failure to

buckle up can be a very strong negotiating point for the defendant's insurance carrier.

On the other hand, sometimes the issue of seatbelts isn't even raised. For instance, if a car is totaled in an accident, there isn't much of a defense in claiming that a passenger was not wearing a seatbelt. After all, there's only so much a seatbelt can do. Another obstacle to this defense is that often juries don't like to, in effect, blame the victim, especially when he has been seriously injured. As a result, the seatbelt–comparative negligence issue has limited value in some cases.

Another question concerning seatbelts that might be raised in a trial is whether there is a duty on the part of the driver to see to it that all passengers are wearing seatbelts. Again, this is a matter for a jury to decide. But what if, for some reason, the seatbelts in the car are unusable, either because they are in disrepair or because they have been intentionally put out of commission? If this is the case, the owner of the car, who has an obligation to see to it that the vehicle is in proper working order, may be judged negligent in the maintenance of his vehicle.

Recently, some states, California among them, have passed laws concerning the mandatory use of approved car seats for children up to a certain weight (in California, it's forty pounds). In the event of an accident, failure to have provided such a seat may result in a child having a cause of action for negligence against a parent.

Going with the Flow

Three teenage sisters were passengers in a car driven by the parent of a friend. None of them was wearing a seatbelt. As they were moving down the highway a tire blew and the car flew out of control, swerved off the road, and hit a tree. The driver and all three sisters were injured. The injuries to the sisters were in the facial area and resulted in scarring.

The parents of the three girls retained us to represent them. Initially, we believed the accident might have been due to a defective tire, so the attorney had this possibility checked out. The expert we hired found that there was nothing inherently wrong with the tires, other than that they were low on air pressure. At this point, the attorney had to change her strategy. Instead of suing the tire manufacturer for producing a defective product, she instituted a suit against the driver of the car for failure to maintain the proper air pressure. The case was settled and the insurance company paid the policy limit of fifty thousand dollars.

Frankly, Sir, I Believe You Could Do with a Little Refresher Course

Philip had recently reached the age of seventy and his driver's license had expired. Because of his advanced age, the Motor Vehicle Department of his state required him to take a road test. On the appointed day, Philip showed up at the Motor Vehicle Department and Steve was assigned to administer the test. They got into the car and hooked on their seatbelts, and Steve asked Philip to start the engine. Philip flipped the car into reverse, then quickly floored the accelerator, and the car went flying into the side of the DMV building.

Steve sustained a serious neck sprain and retained one of our attorneys to handle his case. Our attorney argued that even though Steve might have assumed some of the risk because he was, after all, a road tester, Philip was negligent well beyond what any reasonable DMV road tester could anticipate as a normal error; that is, he threw the car into reverse when it should have been moving forward.

Our attorney's argument prevailed, and Steve was awarded twelve thousand dollars in damages. Philip is now availing himself of public transportation.

FAILURE TO MAINTAIN AUTOMOBILE PROPERLY; DEFECTIVE PARTS

As a driver, you have the duty to maintain your vehicle in good operating condition. If you don't, you open yourself up for liability if there is an accident as a result of your failure to do so. But there may also be instance when mechanical failures lead to accidents for which you cannot be held responsible. These failures may come as a result of manufacturer's defects. If this is the case, instead of seeking damages from the driver, the person injured in the accident stands a better chance of collecting by going after the manufacturer or whoever was responsible for the faulty equipment.

Here are a few examples of the cases we have had in which defects or failure to properly maintain a vehicle have come into play.

Better Seen and Not Heard

Mary, who suffered from epilepsy, was driving home with her twelve-year-old son David in the car. Suddenly, she lost control of the car and it smashed into a brick wall. Both Mary and her son suffered several broken bones. Later, when questioned by the police, she couldn't remember what happened. She said, "I guess I had a seizure." David said, "Mom, the car just went out of control."

While Mary and her son recuperated in the hospital, the car was taken to a local garage to be repaired. In examining the car, the mechanic noticed that hanging loose from the bottom of the chassis was a tie rod, which is part of the steering mechanism and is held in place by a cotter pin. The mechanic noticed that the rod was hanging loose on one end, but was still attached on the other end. When Mary's husband came in to check on the progress of the repairs, the mechanic told him, "I know why your wife lost control of the car. The tie rod wasn't properly in place."

At this point, Mary's husband went to an attorney in one of our offices and asked him to handle the case. The attorney visited the mechanic and questioned him about the tie rod. "It's important to know that if the tie rod came loose as the result of a crash," the mechanic explained, "it would have actually broken off. But in this case, the cotter pin connecting it just fell out."

The attorney then checked with Mary's husband and found that only six months before an automotive shop had replaced that tie rod. Evidently, it had been improperly installed and, according to the mechanic, over time the vibrations of the car caused the cotter pin to come loose and eventually fall out, allowing the tie rod to become disconnected. That explained why the car suddenly went out of control. With this information, the attorney then instituted a suit against the automotive repair shop, which eventually settled the action for sixty thousand dollars.

What was particularly interesting in this case was that if the mechanic hadn't found that loose tie rod, it would have been very difficult for Mary to collect, simply because of the statement she made at the time, which appeared in the police report: "I guess I had a seizure." This points out how important it is not to make any kind of statement accepting guilt or blame for an accident. In this case, the accident wasn't caused by Mary's having a seizure, but rather by an improperly installed part.

Hitting the Brakes

Joe was driving down the street. Ahead of him, three cars had just stopped for a red light. Seeing them, Joe hit the brakes in what he thought was plenty of time, but his car did not respond. As a result, he smashed into the car closest to him. That car hit the one in front it, which, in turn, hit the one in front of it, causing damage to all four cars.

Joe came to one of our attorneys, claiming that his brakes were defective and that that had caused the accident. After investigating his claim, our attorney found that Joe had, in fact, just weeks before had a brake job done at a local garage. The attorney had the car checked out by another mechanic, who offered the opinion that the brakes had been improperly repaired. Consequently, Joe sued the local garage for failure to repair his brakes properly. Just before the case was scheduled to go to trial, the garage's insurance company settled the claim for seventeen thousand dollars.

This case points out that an attorney must be flexible. If one theory of liability doesn't work out, he must seek another one that might. In other words, he must not only be very much aware of the facts of the particular case, he also must be willing to shift gears. Take the following case, for instance. George was walking down a city street, reached the curb, saw that the light was with him, and began to cross. However, at the same time there was a traffic officer directing cars. Despite the fact that the light was in George's favor, the traffic officer waved a car through the intersection. It hit George and injured him seriously. Whom would he sue? Was the driver acting negligently? Maybe not, since he was only following the directions given by the traffic officer. Instead, George's attorney would probably sue the city for the negligence of the traffic officer, or both the city and the driver.

AUTOMOBILE COLLISIONS

In today's crowded streets and stop-and-go traffic, rear-end collisions are quite common. For the most part in these accidents, it is the driver of the vehicle that rear-ends the other vehicle who is responsible for the accident. However, there are some exceptions, including the following cases that we have handled.

Man's Best Friend

Mary was driving her car down a country road when she saw a dog dart in front of her. She quickly stepped on the brakes to avoid hitting the dog and, as a result, the car behind her, driven by Dave, rear-ended her. Dave suffered head injuries, as well as whiplash. Dave retained one of our attorneys, who, after investigating the case, decided not to seek damages from Mary, but rather from the owner of the dog. This decision was made because it was found that the dog's owner had a habit of letting his dog run free. The argument our attorney made was that the owner should have known that this could present a hazard and, consequently, he acted negligently by allowing his dog to run loose.

This argument prevailed and Dave was able to collect damages on the dog owner's homeowner's policy. However, Dave was comparatively negligent in this case, because he was driving too close to Mary's vehicle when it suddenly braked.

Whiplash is a frequent injury in rear-end collisions. Most people hardly even believe this injury exists until it happens to them. It's an injury that doesn't really show up well in X-rays and other medical tests. As a result, it's very hard for your attorney to convince a jury that you are suffering from this injury. But the injury is real. Just ask anyone who has experienced it.

The fact is, 75 percent of the injuries we see in our practice are soft-tissue injuries—that is, whiplash, lower back strain or sprain, or other muscle-related damage. Commonly, these injuries require four to nine months of medical or physical therapy. The best way to deal with whiplash is to see a doctor immediately after an accident and get continued and well-documented treatment. In the end, however, it will be up to you and your attorney to convince a jury that your injury is as real and as debilitating as one they can see on an X-ray.

Off the Beaten Path

Late one evening, Dennis was driving his car down a street in Los Angeles. When he slowed down to stop for a light, he was rear-ended. Before he could get out of his car to check on the damage, the car that had hit him pulled away. However, the license plate fell off the vehicle. Dennis picked it up, looked at it, and then began waving it at the car that had hit him as it moved further and further away. Suddenly, the other car made a U-turn and came back to the scene of the accident. Four men jumped out of the car and grabbed the plate from Dennis, beat him up, and then left him there. Fortunately, he had memorized the license plate number.

As it turned out, most of Dennis's injuries came not from the collision, but from the beating he sustained. When his insurance company refused to pay for his injuries, because they said they didn't come as a result of the accident, Dennis hired an attorney in one of our Los Angeles offices. Our attorney argued that the injuries Dennis suffered did, in fact, arise out of a continuing incident that began with the collision and that therefore the insurance company was liable to pay for those injuries. Using this argument, our attorney was eventually able to settle the case for twelve thousand dollars.

The Sympathy Factor

No matter how good your case might seem, there are some times when you must settle for a lesser amount than you think you're entitled to, simply because of circumstances. The case that follows is a good example of just that kind of situation.

Joseph was fourteen years old and having trouble at home. He decided to run away. One night, while his parents were asleep, he sneaked out to the garage and stole his mother's car. He picked up his fifteen-year-old friend Bobby, and with Bobby at the wheel, they headed from Arizona to Colorado. It was winter. The roads were icy. The highway was practically empty and Bobby was pushing ninety miles an hour. The car hit a patch of ice. Bobby lost control of the car and it hit an abutment. Joseph was killed instantly, but Bobby walked away without a scratch. One of our attorneys was hired by Joseph's parents to sue Bobby for negligence.

In the meantime, Bobby had been tried, convicted, and was doing time for vehicular manslaughter. The attorney went to the prison to take Bobby's deposition and found that he was an emotional wreck. Filled with sorrow and remorse for what happened to his friend, he could hardly talk. After completing the deposition, the attorney walked away and said to himself, "There's no way I'm going to take this to trial. If the other side puts Bobby up on the stand, a jury's going to feel ten times more sorry for him than they are for my clients, especially since Joseph was running away from home because he was having so much trouble there."

This case is a good example of how both an attorney and a client have to be aware not only of the facts surrounding an accident, but also the nuances of the case. Sometimes, an attorney has to go to his client, who is the injured party, and say that yes, the other party was at fault, but he will get a good deal of sympathy too, and for that reason a trial might go badly for you. That was just what our attorney did and, fortunately, Joseph's family agreed with him and we were able to reach what we thought was, under the circumstances, a fair settlement, without having to put both sides through what could have been a wrenching emotional experience.

DRUNK DRIVING

One Too Many for the Road

Jerry and Eddie, two college wrestlers who were celebrating a recent victory, were driving a cargo van to Lake Tahoe where they were planning to spend their school vacation. They had been drinking heavily, making several stops along the way in bars and at grocery stores where they picked up more beer to drink on the trip. Eddie was driving when the van went up on a snowbank and rolled over. At the time, Jerry was sitting on top of a cooler of beer that was in the middle of the van. Eddie was virtually unhurt, but Jerry was crushed against the roof and was rendered quadriplegic.

Jerry retained one of our attorneys to represent him. The attorney proceeded on two fronts. First, he filed a claim against the manufacturer of the van, maintaining that the roof was defective in that it wasn't made strong enough to withstand the crash. The other cause of action was filed against the various grocery stores and bars along the way for serving alcohol to obviously intoxicated patrons. This claim was filed as the result of what in many states is called a "guest," a "host," or a "dram shop" statute, wherein the host, whether it be a tavern owner, store owner, or even a private citizen (in some states social hosts are exempted from these statutes), is held responsible for serving alcohol to someone who is obviously intoxicated and who then gets into or causes an accident. If an attorney proceeds with this argument, however, he must establish to what degree every person or bar owner is at fault in order to show who is ultimately responsible. This is not an easy task and it often requires heavy investigation, a host of witnesses, and expert testimony.

As for the claim against the manufacturer, the jury found against Jerry, primarily because he had been seated on the cooler rather than on the seat. Consequently, the jury felt that the position he was sitting in, rather than any defect in the roof, added to the seriousness of his injury. But in the claim against the various grocery stores and bars along the way, Jerry was more fortunate. The jury ruled in his favor and he was able to collect damages in the amount of five hundred thousand dollars, prorated among several defendants. This figure reflected a portion of what the jury determined would be future earnings lost to Jerry because of the accident.

. . .

This case brings up an interesting point concerning damages. The same injury suffered by different people may well result in different recovery figures. For instance, someone in his early twenties, with a lifetime of earning power in front of him, could expect a larger verdict or settlement for an incapacitating injury than could someone in his late fifties who suffers the same injury. Consequently, who and what you are are major factors in how much you may receive as an award.

MOTORCYCLE ACCIDENTS

Our experience has been that personal injury cases involving motorcycles and, to some extent, bicycles are more difficult to win, primarily because there seems to be a prejudice against people who ride these vehicles. They are more dangerous than cars, and juries perceive their riders as intentionally taking risks. Many states have now enacted "helmet" laws, which require the wearing of a helmet when riding a motorcycle or bicycle. If you were involved in an accident and were not wearing a helmet, you may be found to be comparatively negligent.

A Case that Stinks

Ron was riding his motorcycle in the vicinity of a riding stable. The horses from the stable, which was a couple of blocks from a park, had to cross two streets to get to the riding path in the park. During their trek, manure was dropped onto the street. On this particular afternoon, Ron was going down this street, well within the posted speed limit, when his motorcycle hit some of the horse manure and skidded into a streetlamp. He broke two bones in his left forearm and his motorcycle was totaled.

Ron asked one of our attorneys to represent him. The attorney maintained that the stable, which was certainly aware that the manure was in the roadways, had the responsibility to clean up after its horses. The defense's claim was that this was simply a naturally occurring situation and that the stable did not have the responsibility to clean up the manure.

This was a particularly difficult case. The plaintiff was a motorcyclist, and if it had gone to trial, it might have come down to whether the jury was sympathetic with the plaintiff. Fortunately, the defendant's insurance carrier decided to settle. Although its offer may have been a bit on the low side, considering the injuries and other elements of damages, our attorney felt that it was the best the plaintiff could do under the circumstances. Going through litigation would have been a roll of the dice and wasn't worth it.

The Wild One

Bobby was out for a ride down a well-traveled two-lane highway on his motorcycle. It was a beautiful, clear day and, lost in a reverie, he was admittedly going sixty-five miles an hour in a fifty-five-mile-an-hour zone. Ahead of him, around a curve beyond which Bobby could not see, on the shoulder of the road, was Cliff, who was in one car of a group of cars that were going to a party. Suddenly, the cars began to make a U-turn in the middle of the road. As Cliff made his turn Bobby came around the curve and couldn't avoid Cliff's car. Consequently, he hit the car and suffered two broken arms. The police arrived and arrested Bobby as the cause of the accident.

This was a very complex case, probably complicated even further by the fact that Bobby was riding a motorcycle and had to deal with a bias against these vehicles. The drivers of the cars were making a legal turn, *if* it was clear and safe. But the argument made by our attorney, who was representing Bobby, was that it was not safe to make such a turn because of the curve that hid the view from oncoming drivers.

The defense, of course, maintained that Bobby was speeding and that this was the cause of the accident. Our attorney could probably have countered that argument by asking the jury to take into account common usage; that is, that five or ten miles over the speed limit does not really constitute reckless driving, and that a slight difference in speed wouldn't have affected the occurrence of the accident.

A jury could have made any one of several findings if the case had gone to trial. For instance, they could say, "Yes, Bobby was speeding, but if Cliff hadn't been making an unsafe U-turn, there wouldn't have been an accident." Therefore, they might have found that Cliff was substantially at fault. On the other hand, they might have found that Bobby's speeding was the substantial cause of the accident.

Either way, it was a case in which comparative negligence would probably reduce any award that Bobby might get. Consequently, when a settlement offer of fifteen thousand dollars came in from Cliff's insurance company, our attorney advised that Bobby take it, which he did.

BICYCLE ACCIDENTS

As with motorcycles, bicycle accidents are difficult cases to handle because of a bias against those who ride them. Many people who drive automobiles think of bicyclists as nuisances on the road, as do many people who live in cities and have to dodge messengers riding bicycles.

One of the questions that often comes up concerning bicyclists is, Are they pedestrians or are they traffic? Although bicyclists often think they should be treated like pedestrians, in most jurisdictions, bicycles are considered traffic and bicyclists are expected to follow the rules that apply to motor vehicles. Consequently, where they are considered vehicular traffic, they should not be able to make a claim based on a statute in force in most states that requires motor vehicles to yield the right of way to a pedestrian.

The Case of the Moveable Bench

Cory, twelve years old, was riding his bicycle on the sidewalk of a main street going through his local town. He was riding near the edge of the sidewalk when he came to a bus stop bench that blocked his path. Consequently, he veered out onto the street and was hit by a car, which knocked him off his bicycle. Upon hitting the ground, he broke his wrist.

His parents retained one of our attorneys to represent Cory.

Our attorney didn't believe he had a good case against the motorist who hit Cory, simply because Cory had suddenly driven onto the street, not giving the driver an opportunity to see him. So the attorney had to see if he could come up with another theory of recovery.

Upon investigation, the attorney discovered that it was a town policy that the bench Cory had tried to avoid had to be a certain distance back from the curb to allow safe passage by a wheelchair. It wasn't and, as a matter of law, it was irrelevant that this accident was different from the kind the rule was originally put in place to protect against. The attorney also found that it was known to city employees that the bench was moved around constantly by the kids who attended a nearby school. So he decided to sue the town for not having the bus stop bench anchored down in the proper place.

The case went to trial and our attorney was able to convince a jury that it was, indeed, the town's responsibility to make sure the bench was fastened down the proper distance from the curb. When the verdict came in, the jury found in favor of Cory, assigning 85 percent of the blame to the city and 15 percent of the blame to Cory. The original recovery was $12,000, which was then reduced 15 percent, making the award $10,200.

You Can't Always Blame the Messenger

Ralph was working as a bicycle messenger. On his way to deliver a package early one evening, he ran a stop sign and was hit by an oncoming car in the middle of the intersection. Ralph broke several bones in his arm. He asked one of our attorneys to represent him. Ralph's story was that when he reached the intersection, he looked both ways before running the stop sign. He swore that the oncoming car didn't have its headlights on. Thus, it became a case of comparative negligence.

As it happened, the accident took place in a state that had a fifty-fifty comparative negligence law. That means that if the plaintiff is found to be more than 50 percent responsible for the accident, he does not recover. Despite the odds against winning, our attorney decided to take the case. He searched for witnesses and was finally able to locate someone who corroborated Ralph's story that the car that hit him didn't have its headlights on.

The case went to trial and the jury finally came in with a verdict that Ralph was 40 percent responsible for the accident, while the driver of the car was 60 percent responsible. Consequently the award to Ralph, which was for twenty-five thousand dollars, was reduced to fifteen thousand dollars.

Another kind of bicycle accident that's becoming rather common in large cities occurs when a car is parked and someone begins to get out without looking. A bicyclist, caught unaware, slams into the open door and is injured. Is there any liability?

The answer depends at least in part on where you live. When exiting a vehicle in traffic, you should always use some care, making sure that there's no one coming toward you. In some jurisdictions, the person exiting the vehicle might be held liable. However, in a large city like New York, with its congested traffic and its speeding bicyclists, it might be difficult to find a jury that would rule in favor of the cyclist.

Once again, this case points up the impact on a jury's decision of the particular factual circumstances surrounding a case, as well as the particular jurisdiction in which it is brought.

As the cases we have described in this chapter demonstrate, there are many variables when you have a motor vehicle accident, including issues of insurance, liability, whom to sue, your own possible contribution to the accident, and getting the proper medical attention.

Here is a checklist of some of the major things you ought to do if you are involved in a motor vehicle accident:

- Report the accident to the police.
- Remain at the scene until the police arrive.
- Get prompt medical attention, if necessary.

- Exchange pertinent information with the other driver.
- Get the names of witnesses.
- Don't talk about the accident until you have consulted an attorney.
- Keep a detailed diary of the medical treatment for your injuries and time lost from work.

Given the complexity of the issues involved in motor vehicle accidents, it is important to find an attorney who specializes in this kind of personal injury case. If the injuries are serious, it is a good idea to interview several attorneys. Unfortunately, there are some attorneys who are unscrupulous and will say anything to get your case. Beware of those attorneys who make the possible recovery sound too good, or those who promise you the moon. It might be an indication that they are not going to handle your case in a professional manner.

CHAPTER EIGHT

ACCIDENTS TO CHILDREN

SEVEN-YEAR-OLD Johnny was playing hide-and-seek with several other kids in a suburban neighborhood outside a large southern California city. After about a half hour the game ended, but Johnny was nowhere to be found. Johnny's best friend, Timmy, became worried and alerted Johnny's parents, who scoured the neighborhood for him. No luck. Finally, the police were called. An hour or so into the search, Johnny was finally found locked in an empty refrigerator, which was, ironically, sitting in his family's own garage.

Tragically, Johnny was dead—not, as it turned out, from lack of air, but rather from hyperthermia due to the intense summer heat. This disastrous accident occurred because the refrigerator could be opened only from the outside and once Johnny crawled inside to hide and shut the door, he was trapped. After several months of mourning, Johnny's parents, filled with anger and frustration over an accident they felt could have been avoided, finally contacted an attorney in one of our offices, who agreed to handle the case.

Realizing that this would be a product liability case (this kind of case will be discussed at length in Chapter 9), the first thing the attorney did was ask to examine the refrigerator. He immediately noted that it was old—manufactured in 1973—and that it could only be opened from the outside. To have a cause of action for such an old machine, the attorney had to prove wrongdoing, which, in this case, would mean showing that there had been negligent conduct on the part of the designer or manufacturer of the refrigerator.

To prove wrongdoing we had to hire an engineer to research the design of the machine, as well as the design of other similar items that were on the market in the early 1970s. Also part of the research was to unearth contemporary consumer or trade magazine articles that might have brought attention to the fact that there were potential faults in the design of such appliances.

After several months, the engineer handed in his report, which, among other things, stated that even before 1973, the same company that manufactured the refrigerator had been producing clothes dryers that could be opened from the inside. As far as our attorney was concerned, this was proof that the company was building one of its products the right way at the same time it was building another of its products the wrong way. This, in itself, would serve as strong evidence that the company was guilty of negligence, since it had to have been aware that there were problems with the way the doors of its household products were constructed. We also discovered that in 1974, the federal government adopted new standards requiring that dryer and refrigerator doors be openable from the inside. The manufacturer surely knew of these standards before they were officially adopted.

With this information in hand, our attorney was able to negotiate a large settlement, which, although it could never bring Johnny back to life, might at least act as a deterrent to similar wrongdoing and save other children from the same horrible fate.

This case was one of the more tragic examples of the kinds of accidents that can and do befall children every day. In many ways, children are just accidents waiting to happen. What adult do you know who can't point to some scar on his or her body that came as the result of a childhood accident?

The vast majority of injuries to children are the result of unsafe toys, including bicycles, roller skates, scooters, and skateboards. But many of the more serious accidents involve unsupervised play in swimming pools, in playgrounds, on the streets, or in other areas that are supposedly off-limits to children. The statistics are frightening. In 1986, 123,000 children were injured by toys and 390,000 by bicycles. Five children died from choking on balls or marbles. Two were choked or suffocated by stuffed toys.

Accidents involving children are a part of growing up. They happen in the home: Bookcases can fall when a child tugs on them; electrical outlets can be inviting to children's small fingers; the contents of open cleaning product and pill bottles can be ingested; small objects or even food can cause choking. Or accidents can happen outdoors, in streets, playgrounds or backyards: falls from swings; bites from animals; or injuries from being struck by a thrown rock or other object. And it seems that every part of a child, from fingers to toes, is vulnerable. Of course, the majority of injuries to children are relatively slight—lacerations, contusions, and abrasions. But many are far more serious, involving broken bones or even asphyxiation.

With so many dangers out there, our society has found it in its best interests to try to protect children as much as possible. There is no real way to shield a child from all chance of injury, but there are ways to shield them from many types of hazards that are and should be avoidable.

Insofar as various products are concerned, children are certainly more at risk than adults, simply because they tend to be more fragile, careless, innocent, and unable to protect themselves against dangers they often don't even recognize. In fact, under the law, children four years old and under (in some states the age is six, seven, or higher) are presumed incapable of committing negligence, because they do not understand the workings of the world well enough to determine right from wrong, or safe from unsafe. Common sense has been deemed to apply realistically only to adults. It is, then, an adult standard for which there is no juvenile counterpart.

With this in mind, in 1973 the Consumer Product Safety Commission (established by the Consumer Product Safety Act passed in 1972, primarily in response to a finding that an unacceptable number of consumer products presented unreasonable risks of injury) began gathering information on toy and other product hazards and passed regulations and set standards to reduce such hazards. The commission has, over the years, banned various products that present unreasonable and avoidable risks, which include the potential of injury as the result of electrical, mechanical, or thermal malfunctions, strangulation, inhalation, choking, and poisoning.

For instance, in 1986, a small teddy bear was recalled when it was found that one paw held three wires with balls attached to the ends. When the bear was tested by the CPSC, the balls came off the wires, thereby exposing the child to the sharp wire point, as well as running the risk of the child's swallowing and choking on the balls.

That same year, after a one-year-old child choked on a small rubber ball that came as a prize in boxes of Cheerios, General Mills recalled several million boxes of the cereal. And in another action, Avon recalled 350,000 terrycloth bath toys in the shape of a bee, because the antennae when pulled off and swallowed posed a potential choking hazard to children.

In 1988, Fisher-Price recalled nearly 400,000 "Pop-Up Playhouse" toys, after receiving many reports that the playhouse had suddenly come apart, resulting in parts being hurled through the air. Subsequently, the playhouse was redesigned and marketed in a safer version. And these are but a few examples of the changes that have occurred not only because of consumer awareness, but also because of lawsuits that were or might have been filed to make the world a little safer for children to live and grow up in.

Consumer awareness has also forced manufacturers of toys to adhere to a policy of warning parents of potential dangers that are inherent in their products. In fact, if there is a lawsuit concerning the safety of a toy, often one of the primary factors that a jury must take into consideration is whether a manufacturer had a duty to warn of the danger and, if it did, what the scope of that duty was. In order to determine the extent of this duty, the jury may be asked to consider several things, including custom and practice in the industry; the obviousness of the danger; whether there was any knowledge on the part of the users that the product might be dangerous; the likelihood that the user's activity would create the danger; the degree of danger; any statutes and ordinances that would apply to the product (for instance, if fireworks are illegal in a state, that would certainly affect the liability arising from sale of those kinds of products); and finally, the sufficiency of any warnings attached to the product. One of the most common warnings involves toys that have small parts, which should not be given to infants. Furthermore, manufacturers even have a duty to consider any *foreseeable* misuse of their products, and they must provide warnings concerning the dangers that might result from such foreseeable misuse.

THE WAGES OF GRIEF

Perhaps the worst possible tragedy that can befall a parent is the death of a child. If a child breaks an arm or a leg, or even is scarred as the result of a fall or a burn, just compensation may be awarded. However, if a child dies, as Johnny did when he was trapped in a refrigerator, is any monetary compensation large enough? Can there be any compensation for that kind of loss? And if there is, how can it possibly be calculated? These are questions that the legal system has grappled with for years.

In the early 1950s, ten-year-old Tommy Gibson fell down an open New York City manhole and was drowned. In a civil suit brought against the city, a jury awarded Tommy's parents $42,000. At the time, this amount would have been rather routine for a personal injury suit over a lost hand or eye, but it was unheard of for the wrongful death of a child. After hearing the jury's decision, the judge cut the award to $25,000, and on appeal, the state appellate court cut it again, to $17,500.

Contrast this to a recent recovery of $9.25 million that a state circuit court jury in West Palm Beach, Florida, awarded to the parents of three-year-old Leslie Nicole Smith, who was killed by a falling freeway sign. Obviously, we've come a long way in just thirty-five years, although some may not agree.

What has happened is that the courts in many states have ruled that in the case of the wrongful death of children parents can recover for their grief and anguish and not solely for what the deceased child's economic contributions to the parents might have been. In many states, even the economic argument has been dismissed since it was virtually impossible to calculate a child's future earnings.

Some states (California is one of them) still have statutes that rule out parents' recovery for grief. However, while claimants cannot recover for the personal grief, sorrow, and anguish occasioned by the death of a child, they are entitled to compensation for the love, companionship, affection, comfort, solace, and moral support they have lost as a result of the wrongful death of their child.

In New York, you also cannot recover for grief. However, if a parent actually witnesses the fatal injury by being in the so-called "danger zone," recovery could be obtained for emotional distress. Other states have placed a cap on the amount that can be awarded. Nevertheless, the trend appears to be away from this restrictive approach and toward allowing a parent of a deceased child to recover for emotional distress.

A particularly graphic example of this was a 1980 New Jersey case, *Portee* v. *Jaffee,* in which a seven-year-old boy was trapped between the door and shaft of an elevator. Over the course of a rescue attempt that spanned four hours, his mother watched helplessly as her son suffered massive internal bleeding, screamed, flailed about, and eventually died, still trapped. A short time later, the mother attempted suicide. The court decided that these facts did, indeed, support a valid, separate action for her emotional distress.

DROWNING ACCIDENTS

Some of the most tragic, senseless, and preventable accidents involving children occur around water—in swimming pools or lakes or at the seashore. Swimming pools, in particular, are the location of some of the more serious accidents. Made for pleasure, they sometimes are the cause of untold pain. The standard of care expected of pool owners is usually high, yet today, in many jurisdictions (New York is one of them), you are considered to have assumed a risk when you dive into a pool. Consequently, in these jurisdictions it is somewhat more difficult to recover for swimming pool accidents than for other types of accidents—difficult, but not impossible, especially if you can prove that there was gross negligence involved.

Here are several examples of water-related accidents.

Water, Water Everywhere

Mac and Sarah were having a vacation home built in a Pennsylvania mountain resort. The resort was owned by a number of people, bound together by a homeowner's association. This association was in charge of overseeing the facilities, including a golf course, a restaurant, a clubhouse, and a lakeside beach.

One summer weekend, Mac and Sarah, along with Bobby, their twelve-year-old son, visited the resort to see friends and to see about the progress of their house. While Mac and Sarah, along with a group of ten or twelve other adults, were picnicking on shore, Bobby decided to go for a swim in the lake. The swimming area was marked off by buoys attached to a rope and, about forty feet from shore, there was a floating dock. Bobby swam out to the dock and sunned himself there for fifteen or twenty minutes. Then he dove into the water and began to swim back to shore. He was no more than fifteen or twenty feet from shore when he started waving his arms, indicating that something was wrong.

His parents, along with the others on shore, noticed something was wrong, but before they could do anything, Bobby had gone under. The lake, which was fed by underground mountain streams, was extremely cold. A teenager on shore dove into the water and tried to find Bobby. But he couldn't. The water was too deep where Bobby had gone down.

Meanwhile, the fire department was called. Firemen arrived and after twenty minutes they finally found Bobby. Miraculously, because of the coldness of the water, he was still alive, but only barely. In a coma, he was rushed to the hospital, where he was put on life-support systems. After several months of mounting medical bills, Mac and Sarah consulted an attorney from one of our offices, wanting to know if there was any liability on the part of the homeowner's association.

This was a very complex and tricky case. In the state where the accident occurred, there is a statute that mandates that a lifeguard must be present at any resort area. There was no lifeguard present at the time of Bobby's accident. Swimmers are also supposed to be warned of unexpected hazards. There was no such explicit warning.

On the other hand, the homeowner's association could argue that it did rope off the swimming area, which was quite small, and there was even a dock on which swimmers could rest. The association might also argue that it wasn't in a strict sense a resort, but rather a private enclave that had no legal responsibility to provide a lifeguard.

In arguing this case, our attorney would have maintained that the failure to warn of the depth of the lake was negligent, since that depth was, in fact, the proximate cause of the child's injuries, because it made it difficult to find Bobby and bring him back up to safety. However, this case does point out some interesting dilemmas. Let's take it a step further. Suppose that Bobby had been a beginning swimmer, or something had been physically wrong with him. perhaps he suffered from epilepsy. Would that make a difference in the case?

Probably. A jury could rule that Mac and Sarah were negligent in allowing him to swim unattended, which might result in limiting their recovery for Bobby's damages on the grounds of comparative negligence. Bobby's recovery might also be limited by his own negligence, since he was of an age at which a child can be considered negligent if such a finding is supported by the facts.

Eventually, this case was settled for a significant amount.

Bubble, Bubble, Toil and Trouble

Three families were attending a backyard barbecue, including George, his wife Nancy, and their four-year-old daughter Cindy. At one end of the large patio there was a Jacuzzi. To stem the growth of bacteria, an algicide had been put into the Jacuzzi. It was a soapy substance, and when too much of it was put into the water and the Jacuzzi was turned on, an enormous quantity of soap bubbles was created. On this particular afternoon, that was exactly what happened.

The adults were all gathered around the grill, getting hamburgers, while several of the younger children were playing in the Jacuzzi. One of the adults went over to the kids and told them to get out of the water because it was time to eat. It appeared that they all did, but when Nancy looked around for Cindy she was nowhere to be found. They looked inside the house, thinking she might be there. She wasn't. They looked in the Jacuzzi, but saw nothing but a mass of bubbles. They kept looking, even going to a neighbor's yard, but they still couldn't find her. Finally, in desperation, George jumped into the Jacuzzi and that's where he found Cindy, at the bottom, hidden by the bubbles. Fortunately, almost miraculously, she was found before she drowned. However, she did suffer mild brain damage as the result of being underwater for so long.

One of our attorneys was retained to represent Cindy. He had several choices of action. First, he could have sued her parents for not properly supervising their child, as the parents did have an insurance policy that would have covered them. Second, he could have sued the homeowner for failure to supervise properly and for putting the improper amount of algicide in the Jacuzzi. Third, he could have sued the company that manufactured the algicide for not putting proper warnings and instructions on the box. If he decided to take action against the homeowner, the homeowner might, in turn, take action against the manufacturer of the algicide for failure to warn properly.

In this case, the attorney chose the last two options. He sued the homeowner for failure to supervise properly, and for negligence in causing the hazardous condition in the Jacuzzi. He also sued the manufacturer of the algicide for failure to provide proper warnings and instructions. Eventually, there was a settlement by both insurance carriers.

Coffee Break

Failure to offer proper supervision is very common in accidents involving children, especially young children. Recently, an attorney in one of our offices in southern California represented a five-year-old girl in an action against her grandmother, for that reason.

One afternoon, Sue brought her five-year-old daughter Jennifer to visit her grandmother (Sue's mother). Jennifer's six-year-old cousin, Bradley, was also there. Both mother and grandmother were talking while keeping an eye on the two children, who were busy coloring beside the pool. At one point, Sue and her mother went inside to get some coffee. When they returned, only moments later, they found that Jennifer had either accidentally fallen (or perhaps had been pushed by Bradley) into the pool. When they pulled her out of the water, they found that she had suffered a broken wrist as a result of hitting the side of the pool when she fell.

In this case, our attorney was able to collect from the grandmother's homeowner's policy, despite the fact that Jennifer's mother had been there, too. The reasoning behind this was that since the accident occurred at the grandmother's house, it was her responsibility to supervise the area. When she walked into the house and left Jennifer and Bradley unattended, she failed to live up to her duty.

SCHOOL SUPERVISION ACCIDENTS

One of the most common locations where accidents involving children occur is on school property. When parents send a child to school they have a right to expect that a basic minimum standard of care and supervision will be provided. The school is expected to act *in loco parentis,* which means in the place of a parent. If a jury decides that this standard has not been met, then they may also find that in any particular accident there was negligent behavior by those representing the school.

An Eye for an Eye

In a class of fifth-graders, several boys were having a spitball battle while the teacher's back was turned. These spitballs were wadded-up pieces of paper with a hard substance in the middle. Billy, who was not actually taking part in the fight, was hit in the eye with one of the spitballs and, as a result, the eye had to be removed. His parents retained one of our attorneys to represent Billy in an action against the school for the failure of the teacher to properly supervise the class.

The insurance carrier for the school offered to settle for $250,000 which, considering that Billy had lost an eye, seemed somewhat low. However, upon weighing the possibilities, our attorney advised that the offer be accepted. For one thing, the attorney didn't want to risk going to trial, where there might be some sympathy for the teacher's plight. For instance, the jury might have found that it was unreasonable to expect the teacher to have her eyes on the class at all times, especially when it was part of her job to use the blackboard, for which it would obviously be necessary to turn her back on the class. Consequently, the jury might find that the teacher was not negligent and therefore Billy would have received nothing.

After considering the offer carefully, Billy's parents decided to accept the settlement. But let's change the facts a little bit here and see if the attorney's advice might have been different.

Suppose that this was a special education class, with a roomful of "problem" students. Someone threw a pencil at another student and an eye was lost. Was the teacher negligent? Perhaps, because one might be able to argue successfully that the special education teacher, who supposedly has special training to handle this kind of child, should be held to a higher standard of care. And if there were no special education courses designed to handle them, perhaps there should have been. Furthermore, an able attorney might argue that teachers in special education should be aware of the disciplinary problems and be ready to handle them effectively.

On the other hand, an attorney for the defendant might argue that the incident had happened so quickly that it would be unreasonable to expect any teacher, regardless of how much training he had, to be able to anticipate it.

The point, however, is that if the facts in a personal injury case are altered even slightly, it can lead to a different decision by the jury. An experienced attorney knows that and will never attempt to guarantee the outcome of a case once it goes to a jury.

Firing Up the Old Engine—Literally

Another example of a classroom accident came in a recent case involving a group of high school students who were in an industrial arts class, where they were working on a car. The teacher turned his back for a short while and a couple of kids began to "playfully" pour gasoline on the engine. Moments later when the engine was turned on, it backfired and the front section of the car ignited, causing several students to be burned. They sued the school.

If this case were brought to trial, the plaintiffs' attorneys could argue that the teacher was negligent for failing to provide proper supervision. On the other hand, the defense could argue that the students, who were old enough to know better, were negligent in pouring gasoline on the engine.

Once again, this is a good example of how the variables in

a case make it difficult to predict the outcome. In the end, it would be up to a jury to decide if it was the teacher or the students who were negligent (or, if negligence was assigned to both, what the degree of recovery under the theory of comparative negligence would be). Different juries could reach different decisions. In this case, there was a minimal settlement, which took into account the comparative negligence of the students.

How Do You Get to Carnegie Hall? Practice. Practice. Practice.

Jeffrey was a high school junior and anxious to make his mark on the varsity football team. In early August he received a letter telling him to show up for an early practice session a week later.

According to school district policy, football practice was not allowed to begin until the last week in August. However, in order to get around this, something called "captain's practice" was devised by several high school athletic departments in the area. Coaches were not present at these "unofficial" practices, and there was not supposed to be any contact, sort of like a touch football session. But the bottom line was that, although the letter announcing "captain's practice" was sent out by the physical education department, there was to be no adult supervision at the field.

Jeffrey attended the practice and, as he was running through a play carrying the ball, he was drilled by another boy and wound up fracturing his arm, which sidelined him for the entire season. His parents asked one of our attorneys to represent him in an action against the school for forcing Jeffrey to attend the practice when it knew that there wasn't going to be any adult supervision.

In this case, the defense would claim that by attending the practice, at which Jeffrey knew there would be no adult supervision, he was assuming the risk of getting injured. On the other hand, our attorney representing Jeffrey would, in effect, argue that, "First of all, since there was not supposed to be any contact, Jeffrey didn't think he would be hit. Second, if he wanted to make the team, he had to be at this practice, and if there had been adult supervision there, the no-contact rule would have been enforced and Jeffrey never would have been hit." In the end, our attorney's argument prevailed and the school's insurance carrier offered a settlement of twenty-five thousand dollars, which was accepted.

But again, just to show that decisions depend on the facts of an individual case, let's take a look at the following hypothetical example. A high school student is playing on the soccer team. In the course of play, he gets kicked in the leg and sustains a fracture. His attorney claims that the school had a duty to provide shin guards and, if it had, the leg wouldn't have been broken. The case goes to trial. The jury comes in with a verdict for the defendant because they believe that in this particular instance shin guards weren't necessary and that the risk of injury was assumed by the student when he joined the team.

Pumping Iron

Jerry was a high school student working out in the gymnasium weight room. He was using a weight machine that had, as it turned out, been improperly modified by the gym teacher. As a result, Jerry wound up with eighty pounds of weight landing across his chest, causing the fracture of several ribs.

One of our attorneys agreed to handle the case. If the circumstances had been somewhat different—that is, if the accident had been due to a defect in the weight machine—he could have sued the manufacturer. But in this case the machine had been modified by the gym teacher, which resulted in a defect, so he sued the school, instead. Eventually, the case was settled for ten thousand dollars.

Out of His Class

There are many other kinds of sports-related school injuries, many of them involving gym teachers. For instance, we recently brought a case against a gym teacher for negligently matching up our client, a fifteen-year-old, 120-pound high school freshman, with a seventeen-year-old, 165-pound junior in a wrestling class. In the course of the match, our client was picked up and slammed against the mat. As a result, he suffered a rather severe back injury, which necessitated missing almost a month of school.

We chose not to sue the other student (who was, in fact, simply performing as might be expected and certainly not in a negligent manner), but rather the teacher and the school. The teacher claimed that he was simply trying to motivate the younger and smaller student by matching him up against the older, more experienced, larger student. That argument didn't work. The claim was settled for sixteen thousand dollars.

But suppose that the boys had been equally matched in size and experience and the same accident occurred. Would there be any liability on the part of the school? It is unlikely, since the injury came as the result of a normal activity.

Room with a View

Lack of supervision cases don't always involve either a parent or a school. For instance, we had a case involving a couple of young children who were staying with their parents at a motel. The children were playing outside their room and they came across an unattended cart used by the cleaning people to carry their various cleansers and equipment. From the cart, the children removed a spray bottle they thought held water. In fact, it was filled with bleach. One child sprayed it in the face of another child and it resulted in minor facial burn injuries. Fortunately, there was no scarring.

When we took on the case we sued the motel for leaving the

cart unattended. Since the accident did not involve any serious injuries, the case was settled for $3,500. However, if the injuries had been more serious, there would have been more in the way of compensation.

OTHER ACCIDENTS INVOLVING CHILDREN

If you either have children or have the slightest knowledge of children, you're very much aware of the different kinds of accidents, some particularly bizarre, that they can be involved in. Here are a few unusual personal injury cases we've recently handled.

Too Close for Comfort

Ivan and Marissa could not have their son Daniel circumcised in their native Russia. When their son was three years old, the family emigrated to the United States, and as soon as Ivan and Marissa arrived here, they made arrangements to have their son circumcised.

At three, this is a more serious operation than it is in infancy, in part because general anesthesia is necessary. They brought the child to a surgical center where he was put under anesthesia and somehow, during the operation, the head of his penis was cut off. The doctors immediately performed microsurgery and, although it appeared Daniel would be able to urinate normally, it was not certain whether, as an adult, he would be able to lead a normal sex life.

As far as negligence is concerned, this case was rather simple. The chances were that the plaintiff would qualify for recovery on the theory of res ipsa loquitur (*the thing speaks for itself,* a theory that was discussed in detail in Chapter 1). After all, this was a situation in which there was absolutely no action by the plaintiff that might have contributed to the negligence of the defendant.

However, one question did loom large. How was recovery to be evaluated? The penis would always be somewhat deformed, but how much was that worth? What about sexual satisfaction and performance? What about psychological trauma? Such questions would be answered by experts who testified at trial (if the case was not settled), and their answers would be evaluated by a jury, who would then take them into account when deciding the amount of the award. In this case, a significant settlement was awarded to Daniel's parents, to be put in a trust account for him until he reached the age of majority.

You Do Can Just About Anything, Just So Long As It Doesn't Frighten the Horses

Hal and Becky took their two children, Kathy, ten, and Toby, twelve, on vacation to a dude ranch. The two kids, accompanied by an instructor, were riding horses on a designated path. Suddenly, a motorbike roared onto the property and frightened one of the horses, which threw Toby. He broke his arm in two places.

Hal and Becky decided to sue the ranch owner for negligence in allowing the motorbike onto the property. The case went to trial and the jury, using the reasonable person standard, found for the defendant, ruling that this was not an accident that the ranch owner could possibly have foreseen. Consequently, there was no recovery.

However, let's change the facts somewhat. Suppose that the ranch owner also had established a motorbike path quite close to the horse path. A motorbike comes along, scares a horse, and someone is thrown. Would the property owner be liable? Probably, because an accident like this could have and should have been foreseeable, since the motorbike path was constructed perilously close to the horse path.

Dog Bite Cases

Especially in suburban and rural areas, dog bite cases are relatively common. In general, a pet owner has a responsibility to see to it that the public is protected against that pet. However, in many jurisdictions there is what is called the "first bite" doctrine—that is, unless there is gross negligence (perhaps the owner knew that his pet was dangerous and did nothing about it), pet owners are not held responsible for the first time the animal bites someone. After that, they are.

Over the years, we have had our share of dog bite cases. Here are a few examples.

Give This Dog a Bone

Suzanne, eight, was walking by the house of neighbors. Their dog, which had a reputation for being quite vicious, was in the yard, unleashed. Suddenly, unprovoked, the dog bolted toward Suzanne and bit her in the face. The injury necessitated almost two dozen stitches and resulted in some serious scarring.

In bringing an action against the dog owner, our attorney argued that this was a clear-cut case of negligence in that the owner, knowing that his dog presented a clear danger, failed in his responsibility to keep the animal leashed. However, the question arose of how much damage was done. After all, the full extent of the scarring would not be known for some time. And if plastic surgery was necessary, it probably could not be performed until Suzanne was in her late teens or early twenties.

In this case the attorney could either choose to wait to file the case until Suzanne reached the age of majority (this is rarely done, because of the long wait involved), or file it immediately and try to estimate, through the testimony of experts, what the case would be worth. The advantage of filing immediately is that Suzanne's family would be able to invest the money for her during those ten years before she reached the age of eighteen.

What our attorney finally worked out was a payment schedule wherein Suzanne would receive one lump sum immediately and another sum, which would depend on the extent of her scarring, when she turned twenty-one. This case was settled amicably, but if it hadn't been, it would have gone to trial and it would have been up to a jury to decide how much Suzanne would be entitled to. What if Suzanne had been one of those

children who enters child beauty pageants? Would she be entitled to more money because her scarring might put an end to
this career? And what if this incident caused her to be deathly
afraid of dogs? Would she be entitled to any further compensation? The answer to both questions is that ultimately it would
be up to a jury to decide.

And what if the facts of the case were somewhat different?
What if as she walked by the neighbor's yard Suzanne taunted
the dog, thereby causing it to come over and bite her. Would
that have affected her recovery?

Under many circumstances, provocation might well constitute
comparative negligence, or even a complete defense. But again,
you would have to take into consideration the ages of those
involved. For instance, if it was an adult, who should have
known better, who taunted the animal, he would very likely be
considered comparatively negligent. On the other hand, young
children are held to a lower standard because they are simply
not capable of understanding the consequences of their actions.

Other dog bite cases are similar to the following one. A
family brings home a dog from the pound. Several days later,
the father is barbecuing out on their patio. His six-year-old
daughter and the dog are out there with him. He goes inside to
get the food for the grill. A moment later, the little girl comes
running inside. She had been playing with the dog and it had
bitten her on the arm, resulting in a gash that required a trip
to the local emergency room and a dozen stitches. Does the
family have an action? And, if so, against whom: the pound, for
giving them the dog?

This is one of those cases in which there is damage, but
probably no liability. There was no way the pound could foresee
that the dog would bite the child. Nor was the parent likely to
be held negligent for going inside to get the food. Would any
jury in the world expect a parent to watch a child every single
moment? Of course not. Thus, the answer is, no, it is unlikely
that there can be successful legal action.

PUTTING IT IN A PIGGYBANK

One question we're often asked concerning recoveries awarded to children is What happens to the money they receive? In most states, statutes have been enacted to protect these awards by putting them in a conservatorship under the control of a conservator or trustee who sees to it that the money is spent in the best interests of the child (which may mean keeping it in the bank until the child reaches the age of majority).

In California, the money is deposited in a "blocked" account, usually in the name of the parent or guardian as trustee for the child. The money cannot be withdrawn, unless by court order, until the child turns eighteen. Alternatively, and often more wisely, the funds may be structured, assuming periodic, tax-free payments.

If your child is injured in an accident there are several steps you ought to take.

- Make sure your child receives prompt medical attention.
- If your child's injury is caused by a toy or other product, such as a bicycle, you should carefully evaluate the circumstances to see if that product was unsafe. To do this, it is best to consult an attorney who is an expert in the field of product liability. He will be able to help determine if the accident was the result of a manufacturing defect.
- You should also consult an attorney if there is the possibility that the accident to your child occurred as a result of a lack of proper supervision, perhaps in a school, playground, or swimming area.
- Many parents are reluctant to let their children sue them. But in fact, it is a standard way of collecting on insurance. You should review this issue carefully with an experienced personal injury attorney.
- If you and your child are injured in the same accident, you

should also consider the possibility of separate representation, in case there is some kind of conflict of interest.

Finally, we are not suggesting that every time there is an accident you should look for someone to sue. In many situations, there is no liability. On the other hand, there are many situations in which products are unsafe or conditions are hazardous and litigation is called for. The best way to determine this is to consult an experienced personal injury attorney.

CHAPTER NINE

PRODUCT LIABILITY

AFTER HAVING THREE children, George and his wife decided that they didn't want to have any more. They discussed the matter between them and it was decided that George would get a vasectomy. When the operation was performed, George was advised by his doctor to put some ice on the operation site in order to hold down the swelling.

On the way home, George stopped in a drugstore and purchased a chemical cold pack. Once he was back in his car, he followed the instructions on the side of the package and crushed the plastic pack. When he did so, an endothermic reaction occurred, it began to get cold, and he placed the pack inside his pants, directly onto the groin area, which, because of the anesthetic he had been given, was still numb.

With the pack in place, George continued on his way back home. But suddenly, he felt something wet on his thigh, just below his groin. He looked down and saw that the cold pack bag was leaking right onto the surgical site. He quickly pulled the bag out and tossed it out the window.

When he arrived home, he immediately called his doctor. The doctor explained to him that the chemicals in the pack could have caused some serious burns. He told George to get into the bathtub and put as much water as he could on his groin area. George did so and, as he sat there, he watched his testicles swell to the size of a grapefruit. All this time, of course, he was feeling no pain, because he was still numb from the anesthetic.

The next day, after the anesthesia had worn off, George was in terrible pain and the skin in his groin area was severely burned. His doctor advised him to go to the hospital, where he had some of the dead skin scraped off. This painful procedure was repeated on three separate occasions.

As soon as George recovered from his injuries, he consulted an attorney in one of our offices, who, after listening to the facts of the case, informed him that it looked as if he had a strong product liability case against the manufacturer of the cold pack. The cause of action against the manufacturer was for failure to warn of the possible consequences if the bag did break, as well as the failure to inform the consumer of what the contents of the pack were and what to do if they did leak out.

The attorney immediately began to gather evidence. Wisely, as soon as the accident occurred, George's wife had taken photographs of the swollen area. And, although George had tossed the package wrapping along with the leaking bag out the window of his car, he did remember where he had purchased it, so the attorney was able to visit the same drugstore and purchase the same product.

The manufacturer finally settled for $150,000.

According to statistics made available by the Consumer Product Safety Commission, approximately twenty-eight thousand Americans die and 33 million others, almost one-eighth of the entire population of this country, are injured each year as a result of accidents involving consumer products. And these figures don't even include accidents involving products that are not under the jurisdiction of the CPSC, which would include industrial and farm equipment. Most of these accidents, however, are minor—such as cuts and bruises—and they don't necessarily involve defective products.

Basically, accidents involving consumer products fall into four categories:

1. The injury was the fault of the person using the product.
2. The injury was simply the result of an accident, the cause of which was not anyone's negligent behavior.
3. The injury was caused by a product that was in some way defective and that defect was the cause of the injury. Or, to put it another way, if the product had been made safely there would have been no injury.
4. The injury was caused by an unforeseeable misuse of the product and thus· was the user's fault rather than the manufacturer's.

Here we are concerned only with the third category of product accidents; that is, those accidents that result in injury due to products that were in some way defective (the product caused harm when used according to directions), or products that have failed to include adequate warnings of the possible safety hazards of using the product.

THE EVOLUTION OF PRODUCT LIABILITY LAW

Product liability is a relatively new area of the law. A century ago, the watchword was caveat emptor, buyer beware, which meant, in effect, that it was the responsibility of the purchaser to make sure before the product was bought that it was safe. Of course, one hundred years ago products were far less complex than they are today. For that reason, it was not a particularly unreasonable demand that the consumer take the time to examine a product to make sure it was in sound condition before purchasing it. A consumer could sue a manufacturer only if he could prove either negligence or that the product did not live up to its warranties.

But today, is it reasonable to expect a consumer to know if a washing machine or a television set has been manufactured defect-free? Certainly not. For this reason, the law has evolved to a point where the consumer is now protected against negligence by a manufacturer. This protection comes under the heading of product liability.

STRICT LIABILITY

One of the basic tenets of modern consumer protection law is what is known as "strict product liability," which was developed mostly during the 1960s to protect consumers who could not prove what the manufacturer had done to establish either negligence or breach of warranty liability. Ralph Nader, one of the earliest and most vociferous proponents of consumer protection, was, as the result of his crusade for automotive safety, one of the moving forces behind this concept.

Simply put, strict product liability means that the manufacturer of a product is liable for selling any defective product that is deemed "unreasonably dangerous" and results in injury to the buyer or to anyone who uses it. It is not necessary to prove that the manufacturer was negligent. Under this doctrine, all the plaintiff need do is show that the product was defective, that it was allowed to be sold, and that the plaintiff's injuries were caused by the defect in that product. The direct result of this doctrine, which, in effect, is our society's way of policing manufacturers, is that there is now a strong incentive for manufacturers to design safer products. If they fail to do this, they will be forced to compensate users of that defective product for any resulting injuries.

But it is not only the manufacturer who may be held strictly liable. For instance, suppose that you purchase a VCR in Store Y that was manufactured by Company X. The VCR is delivered and you ask someone from your local TV repair shop to install it for you. A week after it's installed, there's a short in the VCR, which causes a fire in your apartment. It turns out that there was a defect in the VCR that caused it to short out. Whom can you sue?

Certainly you can sue the manufacturer, Company X, for producing the defective VCR, but you may also sue Store Y for selling you the unit. Both are strictly liable to you, one for making the unit, the other for selling it to you. But is the man from your local repair shop also liable? Not unless he did something negligent in setting up the unit, which resulted in the short. The reason for this is that the law of strict product liability does not apply to those who are primarily engaged in providing services, such as repairs, installation, cleaning, medical treatment, legal advice, and accounting.

In short, if you were the purchaser or even the "ultimate user" (this may include a member of the purchaser's household, an employee, a friend, or someone who buys the product from the original purchaser) of a defective product, you may sue anyone along the chain of distribution, which would include the manufacturer (even though you didn't buy it directly from that source), the distributor, the wholesaler, or the retailer.

In most states, if you are a bystander who is injured by a defective product, you may also sue the manufacturer under the doctrine of strict liability. For instance, suppose that you're standing near someone using an electric knife and the blade, because of a manufacturing defect, breaks off, flies through the air, and injures you. In this case, because you were injured as the result of a defect in the electric knife, you would have an action against the manufacturer of the product.

In a minority of states strict liability does not extend beyond consumers and users of the product. However, as the injured bystander you might still have a case against the manufacturer if you could prove negligence in either the making or the designing of the product, because sometimes different rules and defenses apply to the same situation, depending on what theory of law is applied.

There may not be liability, however, if the defect in the product was caused when it was unforeseeably altered in some way by someone, including the seller or the consumer, after it left the manufacturer. This only applies to "unforeseeable" alterations to products. But if the alteration had nothing to do with the accident, then the manufacturer may still be held liable.

What Is a Defective Product and What Constitutes Liability?

Generally speaking, there are three kinds of product defects.

1. *Defects that come in the manufacture of the product.* These defects arise when the product is being manufactured, so that it is not made as intended. Perhaps, as might have happened in the case of the short in the VCR, it was miswired, or a part was left out, or inferior parts were used. As a result, the product is not made according to normal specifications and consequently it becomes dangerous.

2. *Defects that come as a result of faulty design.* These defects are the result not of faulty production but of an error in the specifications. As a result, the product is inherently dangerous even though it may be produced in exact accordance with the design. For instance, going back to the case of the VCR, suppose that the wire used was not insulated, simply because the design of the unit did not call for insulated wire. This would qualify as a defect in design, because the plans for the unit *should* have called for insulated, not uninsulated, wire.

The design of a product may also be defective if it fails to include proper safety devices. For instance, inherently dangerous machinery must be designed to protect users from accidents that are likely to occur. This is why automobiles must be manufactured in adherence to certain minimal safety requirements—for example, they must be reasonably "crashworthy." And if they aren't, the manufacturer will be held strictly liable for any injuries that occur as a result of this failure to meet minimum safety standards.

. . .

3. *Defects that arise out of the failure to give adequate instructions concerning the use or assembly of the product, as well as failure to provide sufficient warnings concerning possible dangers from the product.* There must be specific warnings that explain how and why the product may be dangerous, and these warnings must be placed in a position where they can be easily seen by the consumer. However, a manufacturer does not have to warn the consumer of obvious dangers. For instance, a saw does not have to come with the warning that it is sharp and that it may cut someone.

Taking this a step further, a manufacturer may also be held liable for packaging defects. This would include the failure to provide childproof containers, or the failure to take some step to provide tamper-proof packaging.

As far as risks inherent to a particular product are concerned, you may still have a cause of action if you are injured by a risk that you didn't expect to take. For instance, there is certainly a recognized type of risk involved in working with a chainsaw, and you must take care in using it. However, suppose that while you are working with that chainsaw the chain snaps and you lose a finger. That constitutes a risk that you did not assume— the risk that the chain would snap—and therefore you would have a cause of action against the manufacturer.

Generally speaking, the manufacturer is not liable if the product is unforeseeably used for a purpose other than the one it was created for. For instance, in a famous example apparently made up by insurance companies, if you used your lawnmower to trim your hedges and an accident occurred, you couldn't turn around and sue the lawnmower manufacturer for selling a defective product.

On the other hand, even though a manufacturer might claim that a product was not made to perform a particular function, if it is reasonably foreseeable that the product will, indeed, be used to perform that function, the manufacturer might be liable. For instance, suppose that you purchase a chair, which is obviously made to sit in, but when you stand on it to reach a high shelf, it collapses under your weight. The manufacturer can claim that it wasn't made to stand on, and yet if you can show that it is reasonably foreseeable that someone might stand on it, you could well have a case.

Another example is a screwdriver, which is often used for prying. Consequently, a screwdriver should be made strong enough so that it doesn't break and cause injury when used to pry things. However, if you happen to use transmission fluid instead of brake fluid and your brakes fail, you would not have a product liability case, simply because this was not a foreseeable use. A manufacturer need not produce a transmission fluid that can also be used for brake fluid. In short, the manufacturer must be aware of the reasonably foreseeable uses (and misuses) of its product, and take steps to make it safe for those uses by design or by warnings and instructions.

THE DOCTRINE OF EXPRESS WARRANTY

A manufacturer may also be held liable under the doctrine of express warranty. For a plaintiff to recover under this doctrine, the product need not be defective in the normal sense of the word. Rather, an express warranty is created when the manufacturer or seller makes specific promises or representations about qualities or abilities of the product.

For instance, suppose that you purchase an outdoor swing set for your backyard. On the package, it states that the two swings can accommodate up to a total of 250 pounds. You, who weigh 160 pounds, and your son, who weighs 75 pounds, use both swings at the same time. The set collapses and you and your son are injured. In this instance the express warranty offered by the manufacturer, that is, that the set would hold 250 pounds, has been breached, and therefore that manufacturer can be held liable for your injuries under the doctrine of express warranty.

UPDATES IN PRODUCT LIABILITY LAW

Recently, there have been some changes in the field of product liability. For instance, in 1989 the United States Supreme Court let stand one of the farthest-reaching product liability rulings in history. The court upheld a New York ruling that made all manufacturers of the controversial drug DES, which was once widely prescribed in pregnancy and then conclusively linked to serious medical problems, liable for damages in proportion to the national market share they held. This meant that all the pharmaceutical companies who produced the drug would share proportional liability whether or not the particular person actually purchased a version of the drug from that particular manufacturer.

Another potentially far-reaching change instituted by the Consumer Product Safety Commission, effective January 1991, is the requirement that companies report settlements of some product safety lawsuits to the CPSC. This new requirement will help enable that regulating agency to identify product hazards that might otherwise be concealed as a result of secret settlements wherein court records are sealed.

The new regulation involves lawsuits in which the plaintiffs contend that a particular product caused either death or a disabling injury, such as blindness. The regulation specifies that companies will have to inform the federal safety agency when three such lawsuits in a two-year period either are settled or result in verdicts in the plaintiff's favor.

EXPERT TESTIMONY

Product liability cases can be very expensive, primarily because of the number of experts and the amount of time you may need to prove your case. In most instances manufacturers will fight such cases, simply because of the potentially vast sums of money that might be involved if they lose and become liable for all the injuries caused by a defectively designed product. And in many cases, especially with larger companies, they can afford to fight because of the huge resources available to them.

The experts necessary for the plaintiff may include engineers, who may charge as much as if not more than $125 an hour. They review depositions, and in a complex case there may be anywhere from three to fifteen depositions as well as photos, documents, plans, and diagrams used as evidence. Experts also confer with your attorney. This can take many, many hours of their time. In fact, a reasonable, minimal amount you can expect to pay an expert in a rather simple product liability case can range anywhere from $5,000 to $10,000 (and this is before the case even comes to trial). Experts often charge by the day for the trial. In a more complex case this figure can reach $25,000, and that's just for one expert.

Then there are doctors who may be called as expert witnesses to discuss the injuries sustained as the result of the accident. Doctors are often reluctant to testify simply because it takes so much time, time that they feel can be better spent in their practice. (Some doctors are also reluctant to testify against other doctors.) As a result, the price for their expert testimony may run as high as several thousand dollars a day.

Your attorney may also have to hire an economist to testify about the probable loss of earnings you would sustain as a result of the accident. These economists, too, can be costly, possibly even as high as $5,000 to $10,000 for a complicated case. But these experts are a necessary part of a product liability case, not only in establishing negligence but also in helping to establish a figure for damages.

PRODUCT LIABILITY CASES

Like personal injury cases as a whole, product liability cases range from the simple to the complex. Here are several examples of such cases handled by our attorneys.

Tenting on the Old Camp Grounds

Ted and two buddies went on a camping trip. Deep in the woods, seventy miles from the nearest town, they decided to pitch camp. They unpacked their equipment, which included a new tent. Ted's job was to erect the tent. He opened the package, removed the contents, and began to pound a plastic tent stake into the ground using the hammer side of a hatchet.

Suddenly, as he hammered, the tent stake broke in half and flew up, striking him in the eye. At first, it was somewhat painful, but it didn't seem too bad, so Ted just went on with his task. But later, in the middle of the night, he woke up in excruciating pain. His eye was swollen. Immediately, one of his buddies drove him to the nearest hospital, where the lens of his eye had to be removed. Fortunately, with the aid of a lens implant, his vision was saved.

Ted contacted an attorney in one of our offices to see if he could take legal action against the manufacturer of the tent. After listening to his story, our attorney examined the broken tent stake. The original packing had been discarded, but by checking the patent number on the side of one of the intact stakes, the attorney was able to track down the company that produced the stakes. Upon further investigation he found that the company had never done any testing to determine the strength of the stakes. Instead, it simply sold those stakes to the tent company, which then distributed them all over the country. Using this information, the attorney sued the manufacturer of the tent stake and was eventually able to get a settlement of two hundred thousand dollars for Ted.

Although in this case the attorney chose to sue the manufacturer of the tent stake, another option open to him was to sue the company that manufactured and distributed the tent kit for failure to properly test the product before putting it on the market.

How Did You Want That? Blood Rare?

Andy purchased a new charcoal barbecue at a local hardware store. Back home, as he was pulling off the cellophane wrapper, some part of the grill cut his wrist, which resulted in some severe nerve damage. When he visited one of our attorneys he brought the offending barbecue along with him. When our attorney examined the item, she found, by running her finger around the edge, that there was one portion that was much sharper than the rest of the grill. Because of this hazard, she decided that the manufacturer was liable for defective design and she began a legal action.

One of the first things she did in pursuing the case was to see if there had been any other reports of injuries of this kind. She could do this either by checking with the U.S. Consumer Product Safety Commission or, during the discovery process, by asking the representatives of the manufacturer. If there were, in fact, other such injuries, this might open the door for punitive damages, because the company had been aware that it had a product that posed a serious risk to consumers and yet had done nothing about it.

Otherwise, the damages in a case like this would depend on how serious the injury was, which wrist was injured (Andy was right-handed and the injury was to his left wrist, which meant that damages would not be as high as if it had been his right wrist that was injured), how old he was (the younger he was the greater the damages), and what he did for a living (did he work with his hands and would his work suffer due to the nerve damage he sustained as a result of the injury?). In the end, the company offered Andy a settlement of forty thousand dollars, which he accepted.

Going, Going, Gone

William was driving to work one morning in a car he had recently bought at auction. He was driving a few miles over the speed limit and, because of inattention on his part, he rear-ended a car in front of him. In turn, he was rear-ended by the car behind him. William sustained a serious back sprain and consulted an attorney from one of our offices, because he claimed that the injuries he received came as the result of his being hit from behind. As it turned out, when the car was examined, it appeared that there was something wrong with the seat, which had come loose and therefore had a good deal to do with his injuries.

In fact, two months after the accident, William received a recall notice from the car manufacturer stating that there was a problem with the seat coming loose and asking him to make an appointment to come in and have the seat repaired. As a result, we were able to settle the case for $4,500, which took into account William's comparative negligence for going over the speed limit and hitting the car in front of him.

However, this case does raise some interesting points. For one thing, suppose that William had received the notice from the car manufacturer informing him of the defective seat but done nothing about it. Instead, he simply drove around knowing that there was a problem. If he had gotten into the accident under those circumstances, would he be able to recover? Very possibly not, or at least not in full, since a jury might decide that he had assumed the risk, since he had known about the problem but had done nothing to rectify it.

However, let's say William called and made an appointment to have the seat repaired and the first available appointment was two weeks later. In the interim, since he needed the car to get to and from work, he drove it, got into an accident, and the seat was responsible for an injury to him. Would he be able to recover? Again, it would be up to a jury, but the answer is probably yes, because he had made a good-faith effort to fix the problem. The key here would be reasonableness. Was it reasonable to expect that William should not drive his car for two weeks? A jury might well decide that it was not reasonable and therefore William would be able to recover damages.

Let's add another ingredient to the pot. Suppose that William bought the car and, because he was rather handy, he modified the seat somewhat. An accident occurred and the injuries he sustained could be traced directly to a problem caused by his alterations to the seat. Since the manufacturer had admitted a defect in the seat, can he recover? Probably not, simply because the real cause of injury was the modifications William made, not the defect caused by the car manufacturer.

Fire Away

Adam, eighteen years old, was working on his car in the driveway of the house where he and his parents lived. Specifically, he was working on the area around the gas tank. He had a pack of matches in his pocket and suddenly, apparently without reason, a fire started in his pocket and ignited the gas tank. There was an explosion, and Adam sustained some serious facial burns, which left scarring. Consequently, he required several plastic surgery procedures.

Later, when his father went through Adam's pants pockets, he found the pack of matches and noticed there was something odd about them. The striking surface that was supposed to be on the outside of the pack was on the inside, against the matchheads. Obviously, this was what caused the accident: As the matches rubbed against the striking surface they ignited. This manufacturing defect made it relatively easy to collect a $120,-000 settlement from the company that made the matches.

Broken Dreams

Edward was involved in an automobile accident that resulted in serious damage to his groin area. As a result, he needed a penile implant. The operation was performed but a day later, the implant broke and Edward had to return to the hospital to have it removed and replaced. It is common practice during this kind of implant surgery, especially when it involves relatively new products, for a representative of the manufacturer to be on hand to help the surgeon if there is any problem. When the penile implant was removed, the manufacturer's representative immediately stepped in, took the broken implant, and whisked it away.

The implant was not replaced, and Edward had to be sewn up and rescheduled for another operation. Already, he had suffered the trauma and pain of one surgery and now he would have to go through it a second time. He came to one of our attorneys to see if we could help him.

Unfortunately, the evidence was gone. However, after researching the situation, our attorney found that there were other reports of defective manufacture of these penile implants. Armed with this information, he was able to get the manufacturer to offer a settlement of fifty thousand dollars.

If you or someone in your family has been injured by a defective product, you should take the following steps:

- Seek immediate medical attention.
- Keep the defective product, along with any packaging and instructions.
- Note where and when the product was purchased.
- Take photographs of the product and of the injury.
- If you are injured by what you believe was a defective product, it is important to discuss the matter with an attorney experienced in the area of product liability.

CHAPTER TEN

PREMISES LIABILITY

ONE AFTERNOON, RUTH and her two young children were shopping in a local shoe store. While she browsed, the store manager presented both children with lollipops. Ruth finished shopping, paid for the items she had bought, and then she and the children headed out to the parking lot. When she reached her car, she realized her children's faces were sticky from sucking on the lollipops. Leaving them in the car to wait for her, she went back into the store to moisten a handkerchief with which to clean their faces.

Once inside, Ruth found a water fountain and wet her handkerchief. On her way out of the store, as she walked past a large potted plant, she slipped on a pool of water that had collected beside the base of the plant. She fractured her arm and also sustained a serious injury to her back. Ruth retained one of our attorneys to sue the owner of the shop for negligence in allowing a dangerous condition to exist on the premises.

Upon investigation, it turned out that the store regularly placed foil plates under the plants to catch any excess water. After a while, these plates, which cost less than a quarter apiece, would become worn and bent out of shape. However, rather than replace them with new ones, the storeowner would simply reform the old ones and put them back in place. As a result, they had a tendency to crack, eventually allowing water to spill out onto the floor.

When this practice, which clearly amounted to negligence on the part of the store, was brought to the attention of its insurance carrier, the company decided to settle and Ruth was awarded thirty thousand dollars.

Ruth's injury is a typical example of a premises liability slip-and-fall case. It demonstrates the underlying principle of this kind of legal action, namely, that a land or property owner has a general duty of care to prevent injury to anyone who comes onto his property by eliminating any dangerous conditions that might exist.

These dangerous conditions fall into two categories:

1. Conditions that are open and obvious.
2. Hidden conditions that are unforeseeable and undiscovered.

In the past, the degree of care for which the property owner was responsible depended in part upon the reason for which the person injured came on the property. Historically, there were four categories of visitors.

1. *The business invitee.* This was someone who came onto the property to do business with the owner or any member of his family or his employees. The duty of the property owner was to see to it that the business visitor was not exposed to any dangers that would cause him harm. Not only was there the duty to protect the business visitor from any hazardous conditions, but there was also the duty to inspect the premises regularly for such hazardous conditions.

2. *The social guest.* Traditionally, the level of care due a social guest, that is, someone who is on the property by explicit or implicit invitation of the owner, was not as high as the level due to a business invitee. The principle behind this lesser duty is that the owner of the property should not be more responsible

to his social guests than he is to members of his own family. In other words, by coming onto the property, the social guest assumed the same risk as did members of the household. Under this rule of law, the owner of the property was only held responsible if the guest was injured by affirmative acts of gross negligence.

For instance, suppose that you invite someone over to your house. You have a sunken living room, two steps down. Your guest has never been to your house before, and as you hang up his coat, he steps into the living room and, since he is unaware of the two steps, he falls. Under these circumstances, he would probably not be able to recover from you for any injuries he sustained.

3. *Licensees.* These are people who are allowed by the owner to come onto their property for their own benefit or convenience—for instance, allowing someone to take a shortcut across your property to get to their property. The property owner is not required to take any extra precautions for a licensee's safety. In other words, the licensee must accept the premises with all the existing risks. However, the property owner is responsible for any affirmative acts or known dangers that result in injury to the licensee. This would include construction work being done without the licensee's knowledge.

4. *Trespassers.* These are people who come onto private property without the permission of the owner. Traditionally, since they were on the property without permission and therefore at their own risk, they were not due any special duty of care by the owner. However, the property owner may not place any traps or devices on his land meant to injure trespassers, nor can he attack them or subject them to willful or malicious danger. For instance, a property owner may not set up a booby-trapped rifle aimed to go off when tripped by a trespasser. If he does, and the trespasser is injured, he may sue to recover damages.

However, we should point out that a majority of states have done away with these categories and now hold that a property owner owes only one standard of care toward all people, that is, the duty to employ reasonable care depending upon the individual situation.

FORESEEABILITY AND NOTICE

As in any kind of liability for a personal injury, one of the most important elements is whether the occurrence of an accident was foreseeable. For example, suppose that you invite a friend into your home and you are suddenly called away. While you're gone, she wanders into the kitchen and decides to make herself a sandwich. She wants to toast the bread, but she can't find a toaster on the counter. So she opens a cabinet and there, with the cord wrapped around it, she finds one. Unbeknownst to your friend, the toaster has been put away because it needs to be repaired. When she plugs it in, it shorts out, she receives an electrical shock and is injured.

Are you responsible for her injuries? Probably not, since it was not foreseeable that your friend would go into your cabinet, remove the toaster, and use it. However, ultimately, it is left up to a jury, upon examination of the individual facts of the case, to decide what was and what was not foreseeable.

Nevertheless, in many instances, especially in the case of businesses, there is a duty to inspect the property periodically for dangerous conditions and, if these conditions are found, to make them safe. For instance, a supermarket owner has the duty to police the store at regular intervals for possible spills. In fact, some grocery stores have manuals that tell their employees to treat spills as seriously as if they were fires; that is, take care of them immediately. (Interestingly enough, these manuals may be used as evidence in a case, to prove that common practices were not followed.) If this is not done, the owner may be liable for any injury that results from someone's slipping and falling on fallen items.

But even if you do fall on a foreign object or substance, you must still prove negligence, which usually means that you must show that the owner had notice of the spill being there and had enough time to clean it up, but didn't. For instance, suppose that several grapes fall from a fruit bin. The store has a policy of policing the area every half hour. But this policing has just taken place and, only moments after the grapes fall off the bin, you slip and fall on them. Is the owner liable? Perhaps not, since he had no notice of the grapes on the floor and had fulfilled his duty to police the area just moments before. The bottom line is reasonableness.

How can you prove how long the fallen item has been on the floor? You might have witnesses who observed it, or you might be able to tell by the kind of spill: whether it's hardened or not, whether there are substances floating in the spill, whether the water on the floor has been there so long that it's dirty and tracked all around. However, generally speaking, you must be able to show that the dangerous condition was in existence long enough for the owner of the premises to have discovered it, or that it was there long enough so that he *should* have discovered it.

Hundreds, perhaps thousands of accidents are the result of broken sidewalks or potholes. In many jurisdictions, the state or municipality has the nondelegatable duty to see to it that roads and sidewalks are in good shape. As a result, the property owner is not responsible unless he or she has done something to damage the road or sidewalk. In other jurisdictions, it is up to the owner to maintain the sidewalks in front of his or her property.

Some jurisdictions (New York City is one) have passed laws that make it necessary for the city to have been notified of potholes before it is to be deemed liable for any injuries caused by that particular pothole. For instance, suppose that the city is notified of a large pothole that has developed on Madison Avenue and Eighty-eighth Street. Several weeks go by and it's not repaired. At this point, with the pothole getting larger and larger, you go over it in your car, lose control, and plow into a storefront. If you can prove that the city did, in fact, have notice of the pothole, had ample time to repair it, yet did not, you could sue it for damages. However, if the city had never been notified, you might not be able to bring an action.

Liability is also created when a proprietor does business in such a fashion as to create or allow hazardous conditions to exist. This is especially true in a self-service operation. As an example, let's go back to that supermarket. Fruits and vegetables are periodically sprayed with water to keep them fresh. Obviously, there is potential for water spills. In this case, if you fall, you do not have to show that there was sufficient time for the proprietor to discover water on the floor. Instead, it was a condition that existed and the store was required to take special precautions. In short, if merchandise is displayed in such a way that the proprietor knows that spillage will occur, he will be held to a higher standard of care.

There are, of course, some ways that a storeowner can protect himself from liability. One way is to show that he has made reasonable, periodic inspections of an area. Another way is to have called attention to a potentially hazardous condition, for example, by roping off and labeling an area where there has been broken glass.

Another way to protect yourself as a property owner is to make sure that the design of the property is safe. We once handled a case involving a parking lot that we felt was poorly designed because there were no stop signs at an intersection. Our client was injured when his car was hit by another car coming from the opposite direction. In order to bolster our case (which we eventually won), we made videotapes of the intersection, which showed cars speeding through.

PROVING NEGLIGENCE IN PREMISES LIABILITY CASES

One of the biggest misconceptions people have is that simply because they have been injured on someone's property they can recover damages. As with all personal injury cases, in order to collect, someone must have done something wrong; that is, there must have been some negligence or intent to harm. You must prove that there was, in fact, a dangerous condition, the property owner was aware of that dangerous condition (or should have been aware), and that he or she did not take reasonable action to deal with the situation. Furthermore, a property owner has the duty to make that property reasonably safe, but he does not necessarily have to do *everything* possible to make the area safe.

For instance, suppose that you are shopping in a department store. Instead of waiting for the elevator to take you up to the next floor, you decide to use the stairs. On your way up, you trip over your own feet, fall, and injure your knee. Are you entitled to collect damages from the store? No. The accident was simply a result of your own clumsiness.

However, let's change the facts somewhat by adding a foreign object on those stairs, some packing cord, for instance. You trip over the cord and sustain the same injury. Are you entitled to collect? Probably, because the store had the duty to police the area used by the public for just such safety hazards. Even more important, the packing cord, if of the type used by employees, was probably dropped there by an employee, in which case notice would not be an issue.

COMPARATIVE NEGLIGENCE AND THE ASSUMPTION OF RISK

Two important elements often involved in premises liability cases, both of which we have discussed in earlier chapters, are comparative negligence and the assumption of risk. Comparative negligence takes effect when the injured party contributes in any way to the accident. For instance, suppose that you are out roller skating and you stop in a deli to get a soda. You slip and fall over a spill that hasn't been cleaned up. Your negligence in wearing roller skates inside a deli very probably increased the probability of the accident, so you must share the blame.

The assumption of risk means that the injured person knowingly assumed the risk. For instance, suppose that a friend is visiting your house. He hears about the train set you have set up in the basement and wants to go down and see it. You tell him that the stairs are being worked on and that he should not go down. He says, "It's all right. I'll be careful." He goes down and falls on a loose step. By not heeding your warning, your friend has assumed the risk, and therefore would probably not be able to recover damages. In the assumption of risk, however, you must know what the risk is and clearly assume that risk. So, if a floor in front of you appears to be solid, and no one warns you that it isn't and you walk on it and it caves in, you have not assumed the risk.

It should be pointed out that, technically, the doctrine of comparative negligence renders the assumption of risk moot, because assuming the risk when it was unreasonable or dangerous to do so makes you comparatively negligent. However, the assumption of risk is used in the few jurisdictions that still adhere to the contributory negligence doctrine.

PREMISES LIABILITY CASES

Water Guns Don't Wet People, People Wet People

Rosemary had recently moved from North Dakota to Southern California. Her car needed washing. Every day, on her way to and from work, she passed a do-it-yourself car wash. One day she decided to try it. She pulled her car into the stall and, before putting her money in the machine, since she had never used a do-it-yourself car wash before, she carefully read the instructions. The machine consisted of a wand, which first sprayed clear water, then soapy water, then clear water again to rinse the car.

Rosemary took the wand and activated the machine. The water spurted out with unexpected force, causing her to drop the wand. She bent over to pick it up, but the stream of water, which was automatically shooting out of the wand, caused it to fly wildly around the stall. She tried to catch it, but it smacked her in the head. Then she tried to get out of the way as it snaked across the stall, bouncing furiously as it went, before it finally reached her car. At this point, it began to slam into her car, causing many dents and scratches. Finally, the water stopped and the wand was no longer moving. But by this time Rosemary had suffered various head injuries and her car was a mess.

Rosemary consulted one of our attorneys, who advised her that although her accident could be handled as a product liability case, it also fell under the heading of a premises liability action, because it was up to the car wash owners to have known that they had installed a potentially dangerous instrument. The wand should have been equipped with a safety trigger that would not have allowed such an accident to occur. After negotiation with the car wash owner's insurance company, the case was settled for twelve thousand dollars.

A Stitch in Time Doesn't Always Save Nine

We don't always take the cases of people who consult us. In fact, we represent only about a third of the people who come to us with what they believe is a valid case. For instance, recently one of our attorneys was visited by Joe, who told the following story.

He was going shopping in a strip mall; that is, a mall of stores on street level. A couple of the stores were permanently closed, with out-of-business signs in their windows. Joe parked his car in back and, in order to avoid walking around the front, he decided to walk through one of the closed stores, which was boarded up but not perfectly sealed. He managed to crawl through a small opening and, once inside, he started to walk through to the front. However, there was no light and he tripped and fell over something, dislocating his shoulder.

Joe asked us to take his case, but we declined and suggested he see another attorney. We did so because we didn't believe he had a viable cause of action, since the owner of the store did nothing wrong. The place was obviously closed, sealed, and posted. Yet Joe ignored all this and still went onto the premises.

Joe's response to our attorney was, "What if a little kid walked in there?" Our attorney replied, "If that had happened, there's a good chance I would have taken the case." Why? Because the standard of care that the child, or perhaps even someone who was retarded, could be held to would have been appreciably lower than what was expected of Joe, an adult. Since the store was not perfectly sealed, that is, there was an opening through which a child could enter, a jury might have found that the owner of the store was liable. But almost surely that would not have been the case with Joe.

Man Making Call Hit by Dumpster; Film at Eleven

Tom was using a public pay telephone, which was attached to the wall of a building. Opposite the wall was the back doorway of a restaurant, from which employees would periodically wheel a garbage dumpster in and out. As Tom was in the middle of his call, his back to the restaurant, the door opened and an employee of the restaurant wheeled a large dumpster filled with garbage out in front of him. It traveled fifteen or twenty feet and hit Tom from the back. He fell unconscious and was rushed to the hospital.

As it happened, Tom had recently had double-bypass heart surgery. Although his immediate injuries from being hit by the dumpster were basically rather minor, he experienced chest pains. As a result, he became anxious, fearing that he was going to suffer a heart attack. In addition, because he was a heart patient, the doctors felt that he might develop complications because of the accident. Thus, a relatively minor accident suddenly took on far more serious overtones.

All this had to be taken into account when Tom hired one of our attorneys to represent him. Fortunately, the accident had been well-documented by security men who were on the scene and, when the insurance company representing the restaurant first refused to settle, litigation was begun. The cause of action was against the restaurant for failure to supervise properly, train, and educate its workers, as well as for the careless operation of the dumpster.

Tom's health was rather fragile, so our attorney did everything in his power to speed up the litigation process. Within four months depositions were taken and at this point, when the insurance company's attorney saw how strong Tom's case was, the company finally offered to settle. The initial settlement offer was thirty-five thousand dollars, but our attorney was able to get the company to raise it to forty thousand dollars.

Interestingly enough, a healthy person would probably have received a smaller settlement for the same accident. But if an accident aggravates a prior condition, in Tom's case his heart condition, this can be documented and used by the plaintiff's attorney to raise the level of damages, especially if the case goes to trial. This strategy can be expensive, however, since it is necessary to offer expert medical testimony to back up your claim of aggravation of a prior condition. As we mentioned earlier, the cost of expert testimony can run into the thousands of dollars.

Toys in the Attic

Sarah came to one of our attorneys and related the following incident. She had rented a room in a private house. One afternoon, after she had been living there a week, she left her room and began searching for an ironing board. She couldn't find one downstairs, so she went up to the attic to look around. The attic floor consisted of the sheetrock ceiling of the room below crisscrossed by beams. What Sarah didn't know was that in order to walk through the attic safely, she had to step on the beams, not the sheetrock. As a result, she fell through the sheetrock ceiling and seriously injured her back. After hearing the facts, however, the attorney decided against handling the case, primarily because she believed that since Sarah had no real business being up in the attic, there was no liability on the part of the homeowner.

But let's change the facts a bit. Suppose that when Sarah rented the room, she was told that she was entitled to use the downstairs living room and the kitchen. Her first day in the house, she went into the kitchen, opened the refrigerator, and a milk bottle, which was balanced precariously on a loose shelf, fell and broke her foot. Would she be entitled to collect damages?

In all likelihood, yes. Because she was allowed to use the kitchen, it was logical to expect that she would open the refrigerator, and it was the responsibility of the homeowner to make sure that the shelf on which the bottle was stored was securely fastened.

No Good Deed Goes Unpunished

One evening Ted was working as an independent contractor cleaning the floors in an all-night convenience store. While he was there, a young man came into the store and shoplifted a six-pack of beer. The clerk spotted him and tried to restrain the shoplifter physically. They got into a struggle. The shoplifter's buddy, who was waiting outside the store, came in to help his friend. By this time the clerk was being pinned against the counter. Ted, seeing that the clerk needed help, approached and said to the shoplifter's friend, "Why don't you stay out of this?" He reached out and tried to pull the fellow away from the fracas, and in doing so, Ted injured his knee.

Ted hired one of our attorneys to represent him in an action to recover damages. Our attorney sued the store, arguing that the clerk should not have tried to restrain the shoplifter physically, since this was absolutely against store policy. The case went to trial and a jury found in favor of Ted. However, they also made the aggravating ruling that Ted was partially at fault, because he should have known better than to get involved in the tussle. Consequently, the ten thousand dollars they awarded him was reduced by 20 percent.

Truckstop from Hell

Phil was a trucker who made periodic long hauls across the country. One night he stopped at a motel along the highway that catered to interstate truckers. He registered, then parked his truck in a large, fairly well-lit parking lot. Later that evening he had to go back to his truck to retrieve some of his belongings and, when he did, someone hit him over the head with a two-by-four and stole his wallet.

One of our attorneys took the case and, in conducting a computer check through the police department, he found that there had been 160 reports of crime or violence at the motel over the past year. Upon checking further, the attorney also found that the only security the motel provided was one man, dressed in civilian clothes, who occasionally walked through the area. Consequently, he sued the motel for failure to provide proper security.

His argument was simple. Even though the motel did not specifically advertise that the establishment was a particularly secure place, it still had a duty to those staying there to take reasonable steps to make sure that they were well-protected. By its failure to do this, the motel opened itself up to liability. The argument worked. The motel eventually settled for six thousand dollars.

The interesting sidelight here is that if the attorney had not checked and found that there was a pattern of violent crime at the motel, it was unlikely that Phil would have had a successful case. But this history meant that the crime that befell Phil was foreseeable and therefore the motel should have taken steps to ensure the safety of its patrons.

Walking the Gray Slate Road

Edith was visiting her brother at his house. There was a slate path leading up to the front door. One of the pieces of slate was cracked and when Edith stepped on it she fell. She was wearing sandals and her heel was cut badly and a tendon was severed. She retained us and sued her brother for failure to maintain his property in a safe and proper manner. This was a serious injury, but a difficult case in which to prove liability. So we settled the case for nine thousand dollars, which was paid under the brother's homeowner's policy.

But let's change the facts of this case slightly. Suppose that Edith's brother had just purchased the house a few days before the accident. In that case, it could be argued that he might not have been aware of the cracked slate and, even if he had been, it would have been unreasonable to expect him to know about the depression underneath the defective slate. For that reason, he probably would not have been considered liable, since the accident would not have been foreseeable.

Family Feud

Recently, one of our attorneys heard of a somewhat more complex case concerning homeowner's liability. Jim and Sally had been having trouble in their marriage and were contemplating divorce. On a damp, drizzly day, Sally's elderly mother-in-law, Ruth, was scheduled to visit. That morning, Sally noticed that some oil had been spilled on the sidewalk in front of her house. That afternoon, she picked up her mother-in-law and brought her to the house. She helped her out of the car and Ruth started to walk toward the house. Sally neglected to warn her mother-in-law of the oil spill on the sidewalk and, as a result, Ruth, who had trouble walking even under normal circumstances, slipped and fell, breaking her hip.

Ruth hired an attorney and sued her daughter-in-law for Sally's failure to supervise her properly in walking across the property, failure to provide proper support, and failure to warn her about the oil spill on the sidewalk. The case went to trial and Ruth was awarded $100,000. As it happened, Jim and Sally's homeowner's policy was minimal. However, the house was worth $300,000. In order to collect the full $100,000, Ruth had the option of executing a lien on her son and daughter-in-law's house. Surprisingly, she did just that.

In most cases, relatives will not sue each other unless they are certain that there is adequate insurance coverage, and that was what made this case so interesting. A cynic might wonder whether there was collusion between Ruth and her son. After all, a divorce was being seriously contemplated, and if that action went through, Sally would probably be entitled to half the house. But now, due to the lien against it, the house would have to be sold, and Ruth would be entitled to receive her $100,000 off the top, with the rest being split between Sally and Jim. Assuming the house was sold for $300,000, this would effectively keep $50,000 out of Sally's hands. (The $300,000, minus the settlement of $100,000, leaves $200,000 to be split equally, $100,000 each, between Sally and Jim. If Ruth had not received her $100,000, Sally and Jim would have split the $300,000 equally, each receiving $150,000.)

There was no doubt that Ruth's accident was legitimate. However, who's to say that Ruth might have felt like taking advantage of the situation to prevent Sally from obtaining a larger settlement from her son? After all, he didn't talk her out of it.

A Man Doing a Boy's Job

Billy, eleven, had a regular paper route. On a particularly nasty day, his father, Jack, offered to help by driving him around. At one point, they reached a house where the pathway to the front door, rather than running perpendicular to the house, ran parallel along the driveway. Most days, to save time and distance, Billy simply crossed the lawn and dropped the paper in front of the door. But today, as Billy delivered a paper across the street, his father delivered the paper to this house. And taking the same route his son always took, Jack cut across the lawn. However, he never reached the front door. Instead, the lawn over the septic tank collapsed from his weight and he fell in. He suffered soft-tissue injuries to his back and was hospitalized in traction for six weeks.

Jack hired one of our attorneys to represent him in an action against the homeowner. The case is still in litigation, but it raises several interesting questions. For instance, was it foreseeable that the lawn over the septic tank would not support the weight of a man? Would a prudent, reasonable man walk across the yard instead of using the pathway? Did the family that owned the house have an obligation to maintain the land over the septic tank?

Ultimately, these questions will probably have to be decided by a jury. However, a competent attorney would strengthen his case by finding out why the septic tank area collapsed. Was it old? When had it been last inspected? Of course, if it had been the son who was injured, it might have been a somewhat different case. A jury might decide that an eleven-year-old boy would be expected to cut across the property, while an adult should have known better and used the pathway.

Excuse Me, Ma'am, But Do You Have a License to Drive that Thing?

Across the street from a retirement home was a supermarket. Many of the residents of the home bought their groceries at the supermarket and commonly used the carts to bring the groceries back home. In doing so, they had to pass across an asphalt parking lot that was not well-maintained, as there were numerous cracks and crevices in the surface. Consequently, as the carts were pushed they tended to jerk to one side.

Evelyn was returning home from shopping, pushing her cart across the parking lot. She hit one of the crevices, the cart jerked to one side, and she fell, breaking her hip. Evelyn retained one of our attorneys to represent her in an action against the supermarket for failing to maintain the asphalt parking lot, thereby contributing to a dangerous situation.

In order to buttress the case, the attorney visited the site of the accident and, using a shopping cart, went over the same route, video and audio taping the trip, so that it was obvious how dangerous the route actually was. Using this tape, the attorney was able to persuade the supermarket's insurance company to offer a settlement of fifty thousand dollars.

A Walk on the Wild Side

Ethel traveled upstate to attend a business conference at a local resort. One evening, after a meeting, she was walking one of the trails. Although there were no lights, it was a clear night and there were no rules against taking such a walk. At one point on her walk, Ethel reached a bench that was placed a few feet in front of a three-foot-deep crevice. There was no sign posted warning visitors of the crevice or the drop. Ethel sat down, but when she tried to get up, she lost her balance and fell down the crevice. She dislocated her shoulder and severely sprained her knee, causing her to miss three weeks of work.

When she had recovered, Ethel called one of our attorneys and asked him to take her case against the resort for failure to provide proper lighting and to warn visitors of the danger of the crevice. The suit, which is still being litigated, was brought downstate, where Ethel resides. However, it is probable that the defense, arguing that most of the witnesses are upstate, will ask for a change of venue, moving the case to the area where the accident occurred. This may well make Ethel's case more difficult to win, since a jury will be called from among local residents, many of whom themselves depend upon the resort for employment, or at least have friends or family who work there.

Ethel's case brings up the question of venue, or where a case is brought and how this might affect a particular verdict. For instance, if you have a case against a homeowner in an area filled with homeowners who might serve on the jury, they might be more likely to side with one of their own. Or, as we have mentioned before, if you bring a case in a fiscally conservative area, it is likely to have an impact on the size of your recovery.

An experienced attorney, if there is an opportunity to do so, will always try to select the venue that seems most advantageous to his client.

Water, Water Everywhere

One of the most tragic premises liability cases we have ever handled concerned a swimming pool accident. In the past, under what is generally now considered an outmoded principle, there was a theory of law called "attractive nuisance." An attractive nuisance was a dangerous condition that, for one reason or another, was considered tempting and "invited" use by children. Such conditions included, for instance, fences that, when climbed, led to potentially dangerous situations, dangerous piles of dirt or cliffs, or swimming pools that were unfenced or unattended. Under the attractive nuisance theory, the property owner was expected to make an effort to keep children away from danger, perhaps by fencing the property in.

Today, however, the theory of attractive nuisance has largely been replaced by the duty of reasonable care under the circumstances. Generally speaking, if you are invited to swim in a residential pool, the owner is not liable for injuries received while you are using the pool, unless there was an extremely dangerous condition in that pool, which was in some way hidden from you. Then the owner has a duty of reasonable care to repair the condition or warn of it. If you are the pool owner and someone, a neighbor, perhaps, is injured while using your pool without your permission, you are liable only if you caused the injury by doing something extremely reckless or malicious, which might include leaving sharp objects, such as broken glass, in or around the pool area.

This particular case involved a husband, his wife, and their two children. They were visiting a friend's house, which had a pool in the backyard. The pool, which had a black bottom, was half-covered. Leaving his wife and two young children by the pool, the husband wandered away, and when he returned forty-five minutes later he found his wife's body floating in the pool. He dove in and then found his two children, also drowned.

Evidently, one child had fallen in, the other followed, and then the mother jumped in to save them. They had obviously gotten caught under the covering and, because of the blackness of the bottom of the pool, couldn't find their way out. We represented the husband in an action against the owner of the property for not giving proper warning to stay away from the pool. The case was eventually settled for in excess of $1 million.

As a property owner, you have some built-in liability. Consequently, there are several things you should always keep in mind.

- Carefully consider what kind of insurance makes the best sense for you.
- When purchasing insurance, find out exactly what and whom it covers.
- Make sure you are aware of any potentially hazardous conditions on your property and act promptly to make them safe.
- If you are a business owner, make sure someone has the responsibility for evaluating your property to make it safe.
- If you are a landlord, make sure to make it clear to your tenant what portions of the property he has access to.

If you are injured on someone else's premises, there are several steps you should take.

- Get proper medical attention.
- Note what you believe to have been the cause of the accident.
- Take photographs of the area where the accident took place.
- Get the names of any witnesses.
- Consult an attorney experienced in premises liability cases.

CHAPTER ELEVEN

MEDICAL MALPRACTICE

BRAD, FIVE YEARS old, was visiting his grandparents in the country. While his grandmother worked in her garden at one corner of the backyard, Brad was amusing himself by pushing around an old lawnmower. Something got caught in the blades, and when he reached down to pull it free, he cut his finger rather severely. His grandmother rushed him to a doctor, who, before stitching the wound up, gave Brad a dose of chloral hydrate in order to sedate him. However, Brad reacted badly to the drug and, as a result, he went into cardiac arrest. Fortunately, the doctor was able to save him, but for the rest of his life, Brad will have to take heart medication.

After the accident, Brad's parents, suspecting that there may have been some wrongdoing by the doctor, visited one of our attorneys for advice. The attorney agreed to look into the case to see if there was a basis for a malpractice action against the physician. Upon investigation, our attorney found that not only had the doctor clearly injected Brad with an overdose of the drug, but, according to several experts, it was even questionable whether he should have given that particular drug to a five-year-old child. With this information in hand, the attorney decided to file a malpractice suit against the doctor.

In preparing the case, the attorney had to examine closely Brad's medical records to make sure that he did not have any kind of preexisting heart condition that might have led to the cardiac arrest. Once this was established, and a direct link could be made between the administering of the drug and Brad's subsequent heart failure, the case moved forward. After two years, the suit finally came to trial and eventually the jury found in favor of Brad, awarding him $250,000.

In the past several years there has been a good deal of publicity concerning medical negligence, or as it is more commonly known, medical malpractice. The public conception is that medical negligence claims are on the rise and, as a result, the insurance premiums paid by doctors have skyrocketed. The truth, however, is somewhat different. According not only to our attorneys but also to other attorneys we've spoken to, the number of medical negligence claims has, over the past several years, decreased dramatically.

Medical malpractice cases are extremely complex and, as a result, they are difficult to win. It is not an exaggeration to say that suing a doctor is unlike suing any other person on this earth. For one thing, extreme pressure has been exerted by a very strong medical lobby, which has resulted in almost every state enacting rules that not only make it difficult to sue a physician successfully, but also place a cap on the amount for which you may sue.

Medical malpractice suits can also be difficult to win because of the difficulty of getting doctors to testify against other doctors, no matter what has happened. In fact, before 1970, it was nearly impossible to find one doctor who would testify against another. In addition, doctors are less likely than other people to settle a claim against them. Indeed, they typically have the right to demand that their insurance companies *not* settle a case under their special insurance policies.

At the same time, many doctors maintain that juries cannot understand the medical profession sufficiently to come to an educated decision as to what actually does constitute negligence. Instead, they want to be judged by their peers; that is, only by other doctors. Is this reasonable? Can a plaintiff get a fair shake with the decision in the hands of physicians who may someday also find themselves being judged, and who are insured by the same insurance company that covers the defendant?

We don't think so. But in reality only a limited number of personal injury cases fall under the heading of medical malpractice. And because they are difficult to win and are very time consuming, attorneys are loath to take such cases unless they involve serious injury.

A BRIEF HISTORY OF MEDICAL MALPRACTICE

Before the 1930s, medical malpractice claims were rare. It wasn't until the late 1960s and early 1970s that medical malpractice caught the attention of the public. The number of claims against the health-care profession began to increase, and doctors and other health-care professionals complained as insurance carriers raised rates, sometimes dramatically. They also complained about "frivolous" suits, which they claimed were brought without any scientific foundation. After all, doctors reasoned, we can't be held responsible for everything that goes wrong.

In a way, this plea makes sense, since what happens in your body as the result of a medical procedure is not as exact as what happens with a machine that might be defective. Sometimes things go wrong that the doctor has no control over. Should a doctor be held responsible simply because he or she is unable to "cure" a patient? Of course not. But a physician should be held responsible for harm that comes as a result of negligence. And if there is negligence, it should be dealt with in the only arena available to victims, the court system.

Due in large part to this increase in the number of malpractice suits, in the early 1970s President Richard Nixon formed a Commission on Medical Malpractice to study the problem. The Commission's report, issued in 1973, concluded that the escalation in medical malpractice litigation was caused by a combination of two things: Medical care had become more available and was therefore more widespread, and medical advances had led to a growing number of more complex medical procedures.

During this same period, in direct response to the increase of malpractice claims, insurers began raising their rates. Naturally, physicians howled, pointing the finger at attorneys, who, they claimed, were at fault for their escalating premiums. In an attempt to curb the effects of this "medical malpractice crisis," many state legislatures, at the behest of strong medical lobbies, enacted statutes aimed at limiting the liability of health-care providers. These statutes included those limiting attorneys' contingency fees; limiting noneconomic punitive damage awards (those other than medical expenses and loss of earnings, such as for pain and suffering and permanent disability); revising statutes of limitation; and creating pretrial panels to screen cases to establish merit.

However, at least at first, these statutes apparently failed to stem the crisis, since rates generally continued to climb and the number of medical malpractice suits appeared to grow, albeit at a slower rate, annually. And yet the notion of the so-called "medical malpractice crisis" deplored by physicians and health-care providers may be somewhat misleading, especially when you consider the results of a recent Harvard University study, which concluded that, among all the malpractice suits brought, plaintiffs win fewer than half. And of that half, in only 20 percent of the cases that actually go to trial does a jury award damages. Contrary to popular belief, very rarely do plaintiffs win multimillion-dollar cases, and when they do, their injuries are typically so horrible that it's clearly justified.

WHAT IS MEDICAL MALPRACTICE?

Simply put, medical malpractice is negligence committed by a professional health-care provider, whether a doctor, a nurse, a dentist, a technician, a hospital, or a hospital worker, which comes as the result of a departure from standard practice in the performance of their duties and thereby causes harm to others.

Legally, a doctor or hospital commits malpractice when there is a failure to live up to the standards set by the education and training for a particular specialty, or when there is a failure to treat a patient in accordance with the standards of practice in his community (which currently most courts have interpreted to encompass the entire nation, thereby holding a rural doctor to the same standard as doctors in an urban setting).

This does not mean that any medically disastrous result can automatically be traced to malpractice. Many people consider modern medicine an exact science, but it is not. Unexpected complications can and do arise and a medical provider is responsible only for harm that results from failing to use the degree of skill and care used by other medical providers under the same or similar circumstances.

In fact, there are several types of medical practices that, although they may result in injury to someone, are not usually considered negligent. For instance, suppose that you go to a doctor for a serious back condition and, after you have spent several thousand dollars, your condition is no better. Is the doctor guilty of malpractice? Not if that doctor provided standard treatment, for the simple reason that it is unrealistic to expect that particular medical treatments always work for everyone. The bottom line is that doctors are not required to produce results.

Here are some examples that don't qualify as malpractice:

- A doctor is not responsible for detecting impending conditions. For instance, suppose that you go in for a standard physical checkup, you receive a clean bill of health, and the next day you suffer a stroke. Your doctor is not guilty of negligence because it is unreasonable to expect this condition to be picked up in the normal course of a routine physical checkup.
- Providing expensive and unsuccessful treatment for incurable diseases, such as certain forms of cancer, does not, in and of itself, constitute negligence, because it is standard practice to offer this treatment to gain relief from the

symptoms and pain that may result from these terminal illnesses.

- Since the day of house calls is long past, it is not normally considered negligent for a physician to refuse to make such calls, even if that refusal results in harm to the patient.
- It is not usually negligent for a doctor to refuse to treat you. Any doctor has a right to choose his patients and to limit their number. However, once treatment is started, the doctor may not simply abandon you. Before dropping you as a patient, the doctor must give you ample time to find another doctor, and during this time treatment must continue.
- It is not usually considered negligent to order expensive exploratory tests that come out negative, *if* those tests are considered standard practice under the circumstances. If they are not and they cause serious injury, then negligence might have occurred.
- Performing operations or prescribing medication that result in minor harm to the body do not necessarily constitute negligence. In the past, "Do not harm" was the directive of standard medical practice. However, today that has changed. The new standard is that a treatment or procedure is acceptable when the benefits outweigh the harm done.
- *Iatrogenic diseases,* conditions that have actually been induced by medical treatment, do not, under most circumstances, fall under the heading of malpractice. These diseases, which include infections, hypertension, heart disease, acute allergic reactions, liver tumors, deafness, cancer, and cardiac arrest, unavoidably result from the use of diagnostic X-rays, therapeutic drugs, radiation therapy, exploratory surgery, and other treatments and procedures that are standard practice. However, if such a doctor-induced disease or condition should result from nonstandard practice, for instance, excessive use of X-rays, a negligence action may be appropriate. These same rules apply to what is known as *nosocomial disease,* that is, a disease

or condition induced by a hospital. If it is an unavoidable result of an appropriate treatment or procedure, there has been no negligence. If it results from an improper treatment or procedure, that's another story.

On the other hand, there are certain questionable medical practices that may well constitute medical negligence. They would include the following:

- Harm resulting from a doctor's prescribing a drug that has not been approved by the Food and Drug Administration (FDA).
- Harm resulting from a doctor's prescribing the incorrect dosage of a drug, as long as that dosage was not within the acceptable limits of standard practice. Malpractice may also be claimed if addictive drugs are prescribed carelessly and addiction ensues.
- Misdiagnosis of a disease that results in harm to the patient, so long as the incorrect diagnosis is the result of a departure from standard practice or the failure to exercise the skill and ability of a doctor of reasonable competence. For instance, suppose that your doctor diagnoses a pain in your abdomen as only a pulled muscle because he does not perform the proper diagnostic procedures. Instead, it turns out to be appendicitis. Since pain in that area would, in line with standard practice, call for checking the appendix, the physician may be liable for negligence (but only if the condition results in harm that could have been avoided). Also, standard practice usually entails a physical examination before making a diagnosis. Thus, if a misdiagnosis is made over the phone, for instance, the physician may be guilty of negligence. If a doctor is guilty of misdiagnosis, you can bring an action for the harm that results from being given unnecessary or harmful treatment, as well as for any harm suffered as the result of a delay in proper treatment. However, in the case of misdiagnosis, it's important to remember that medicine is not an exact science,

and if the wrong diagnosis is made despite the use of standard tests and procedures, it is not negligence. Therefore, that there was misdiagnosis does not automatically mean that there was malpractice. In the example of the patient with appendicitis, if there is a delay in diagnosis but the treatment is the same as if it had been diagnosed earlier, the only damage might be an extra day of pain—not something a jury usually recognizes as serious harm.

- The failure to perform standard tests. For instance, if someone visits a physician and complains of pains along the left arm and shoulder, failure to give tests for possible heart problems may constitute negligence.
- The failure of a doctor to heed an emergency request might be negligent. By the same token, a hospital emergency room cannot turn a patient away if the problem is serious or life threatening, requiring immediate care. Although doctors are generally free to choose whom they will treat, hospital emergency rooms open to the general public do not have that option. If the emergency room does refuse to treat a patient in a *real* emergency (that is, one that is life threatening), then the hospital may be held liable for damages for any further injury that comes as a result of the delay in treatment because you had to seek help elsewhere. Sometimes the result is death, loss of a limb, brain damage, or other serious harm.
- Unnecessary surgical procedures, so long as these procedures do not fall under the heading of standard practice.
- There are also the obvious cases of medical negligence, such as the amputation of the wrong limb (the left leg, for instance, instead of the right), or performing the wrong operation on a patient.

Other examples of events that may constitute medical negligence are:

- The injection of medication into the wrong part of the body.

- Prescribing medication that a patient was known to be allergic to.
- The improper setting of a broken bone.
- Failure to provide a hospitalized patient with the proper devices with which to summon help.
- Failure of a hospital to provide properly for patient safety (rails on beds, for example).

MALPRACTICE AND INFORMED CONSENT

In 1960, a court decision established the right of a person to determine what is done to that person's body. In part, the decision stated: "A man is the master of his own body and may expressly prohibit the performance of life-saving surgery or other medical treatment. A doctor may well believe that an operation or other form of treatment is desirable or necessary, but the law does not permit him to substitute his own judgment for that of the patient."

Consequently, doctors are required to inform their patients thoroughly about their illnesses and the proposed treatment. Once this information is provided, the doctor must then obtain the patient's permission before treatment is begun. If a doctor begins treatment without obtaining *informed consent,* which is now a standard medical practice, he is guilty of negligence.

Informed consent is still a somewhat vague term, but generally speaking, it includes the physician telling you what's wrong with you; what the proposed treatment is and what it's supposed to accomplish; the chances of success (if the treatment includes surgery, the success-failure record of the surgeon and the hospital should be provided); any and all risks involved, including disfigurement, permanent impairment, or even death; probable side effects, especially from drugs; necessary tests, hospital stays, injections, and so forth; available alternative treatments; the doctor's reasons for believing the treatment he has chosen is better for you than another one; and, finally, the risk to your health should you decide to reject the advised treatment.

In order to be in a better position to give your informed consent, it's always a good idea to obtain a second opinion. Interestingly, most physicians encourage their patients to get a second opinion and today many insurance companies will pay all or part of the cost of having another doctor review your case to see if you require surgery.

One problem attorneys often encounter in medical negligence actions is the lack of evidence of what the physician really explained to the patient in the process of obtaining his informed consent. Typically, the records include a boilerplate list of all possible risks and a note that the patient was informed and consented to surgery. The real course of events may have been very different, but this is difficult to prove.

There are several other features of informed consent. They include:

- The consent must be given freely, without coercion by the physician. For instance, doctors sometimes appear all-knowing and all-powerful to patients, and many patients have a tendency to cower in their presence. Informed consent obtained through the use of intimidating tactics ("I know what's best for you, so just do what I say") is not truly informed consent at all.
- If you are mentally or emotionally incapable of giving informed consent it must be given by a court-appointed legal guardian, who may be either a relative, a friend, or the court itself.
- If you are unconscious and in need of emergency treatment to save your life, a doctor may give you that treatment without first obtaining your consent, as the law assumes that if you had been conscious you would have given your consent.
- Generally speaking, parents have the right to give informed consent for their children. There are exceptions, however, since in some states teenagers may, under certain conditions, give informed consent (the decision to take birth control pills or have an abortion performed are exam-

ples). In all states, however, teenagers can give informed consent on all medical concerns provided they meet one of the following conditions: They live in their own dwellings; they provide for their own living; they serve in the Armed Forces; they are married; or they are either wedded or unwedded parents.

- If, a s a parent of a minor child, you cannot be reached by the doctor, the law permits that doctor to act as the child's guardian.
- Blanket consent forms, that is, forms that give a hospital or doctor permission to do anything they want to a patient, are invalid. Even if you sign one, you could still bring a malpractice action on the grounds that you didn't give informed consent for the specific procedure that caused injury to you.

There is another cause of action that may arise in the medical negligence context: patient dumping, which sometimes causes serious and harmful medical consequences. Dumping occurs when a hospital transfers unwanted patients to another hospital where, because of inferior standards or overcrowding, that patient might not receive adequate care. A federal statute bars this practice and some states, including California, have passed similar statutes.

MEDICAL MALPRACTICE CASES

The Old Hospital Shuffle

Victor, an out-of-work laborer, was walking along the side of a highway when he was struck by a car, causing severe damage to his right leg. An ambulance took him to the emergency room of a local hospital, where, while certain preliminary tests were performed, he was kept waiting for nearly six hours without being treated. Finally, instead of being treated at that hospital, Victor, who had no medical insurance, was transferred to a county hospital several miles away, where he was held an additional four or five hours before being operated on. Unfortunately, by this time the surgeons could not save his leg and it had to be amputated.

Upon release from the hospital Victor consulted an attorney from one of our offices. After listening to his case, the attorney decided to file a malpractice suit against the original hospital for failure to treat Victor, as well as the county hospital, on the grounds that they waited an unconscionable period of time before finally performing an operation, thus causing the amputation of the limb.

This was a difficult case to win. In the first place, patient dumping, which was what happened to Victor, is a controversial issue. The first hospital claimed that the reason it transferred Victor was that it was not as well-equipped to handle trauma cases as was the county hospital. And it explained the six-hour wait by claiming that certain tests had to be performed and evaluated before Victor could be treated.

As a first step in the case, qualified expert witnesses who would testify that what had been done to Victor was outside the normal standard of care had to be found. They would also have to prove that the long delay resulted in Victor's losing his leg. Not only was this a difficult process, it was also expensive, since these experts often charge large sums of money for their time and testimony.

Before Victor's case went to trial, the attorney decided to drop the claim against the first hospital because he was convinced as a result of his research that there was sufficient cause for delay before treatment there. The time may have been a bit long to perform those preliminary tests, but not long enough to, in the attorney's opinion, constitute negligence. Also, the experts weren't convinced that the delay at the first hospital caused the loss of the leg.

But since the tests had already been done and evaluated by the time Victor reached the county hospital, the four-hour wait there before he was operated on seemed unnecessary and the lawsuit was continued against the second hospital. Before the case went to the jury, the county hospital settled with Victor for $450,000.

As Victor was an indigent, out-of-work laborer, his lack of earning power had an effect on his settlement. If he had been a middle-class professional, for instance, he probably would have received a larger settlement because he could have shown that he lost more income as a result of the injury than Victor lost.

Was That With or Without Caffeine?

Fred had been hospitalized for over a week for treatment of a brain tumor. He was being given drugs that not only made him irritable, but caused him to hallucinate. One afternoon a nurse came in and served him hot coffee, which, because proper precautions were not taken, he immediately spilled on himself, causing serious burns to his leg.

After hearing the facts of the case, an attorney from one of our offices felt that under the circumstances the nurse's serving of the hot coffee constituted negligence. The argument was that the hospital, knowing the effects that the drugs he was taking had on Fred, should never have allowed the nurse to serve him something as potentially dangerous as a hot cup of coffee without taking the proper safety precautions. Eventually the case was settled for seven thousand dollars.

Plain as the Nose on Your Face

Lily, who was seventy-two years old, was confined to a convalescent home. She developed a problem in her right leg, which, after a while, turned into an obvious visible infection. Although she was examined regularly by the staff of the home, no notice was taken of her infected leg. Finally, after over a week had passed, a health-care worker recognized the problem and Lily was transferred to a hospital, where her leg had to be amputated. In fact, the infection was so obvious by that time that the doctor who performed the operation told Lily that it should have been taken care of much earlier and, if it had been, the leg could most certainly have been saved.

One of Lily's sons came to us and asked one of our attorneys to handle the case for her. After obtaining the hospital records, as well as getting a statement from the surgeon who performed the amputation, the attorney contacted the insurance carrier for the convalescent home and the case was eventually settled for thirty thousand dollars.

This figure seemed quite low. However, recoveries always differ vastly, according to who has been injured. In this case, Lily was a seventy-two-year-old woman confined to a convalescent home. Would her injury affect her earning power? She had none. Would it severely affect the quality of her life? Probably not, since she was bedridden already. On the other hand, had the same injury occurred to an otherwise healthy working woman of forty-two, who had a good job and many years of earning power in front of her, the settlement would have been appreciably more.

If you are considering a medical malpractice action, there are several things to keep in mind.

- The failure of a doctor to provide a cure for your condition does not in itself constitute medical malpractice.
- As long as a doctor adheres to standard medical practice, he is not guilty of malpractice.
- As long as the benefits of a doctor's treatment outweigh any possible harm, such as side effects, there is no malpractice.

The following situations indicate possible medical malpractice.

- A doctor prescribing a drug that is not approved by the Federal Drug Administration.
- The prescribing of improper dosages of drugs.

- The misdiagnosis of a condition, if that misdiagnosis was the result of a departure from standard practice or the failure to use the skill and ability of a doctor of reasonable competence.
- Any procedure that is not common medical practice.
- Lack of informed consent, which is a standard medical practice.

A malpractice suit is a long, troublesome, and expensive procedure. Such personal injury suits are difficult to win and, for that reason, it is very important that you consult an attorney who is an expert in this field. You must provide your attorney with all the pertinent information concerning your case and then he will try to confirm your version of what happened. Only then, if the facts merit it, will the action move forward.

CHAPTER TWELVE

SUING THE GOVERNMENT

ONCE EVERY OTHER week Steve's job as a private garbage collector entailed hauling old tires and other trash from a truck stop to the city landfill, where he would dump it. The trash went in one area and the tires in another. He had been performing this job for years, but on this particular day he had just returned from a two-week vacation, so he hadn't been to the dump in nearly a month.

Taking his usual path along the roadway, Steve drove his truck and trailer to a hill where he normally deposited the old tires. Then he continued toward the trash-dumping area, up another hill. But this time, just past the crest of the hill, his truck tipped forward and tumbled into a huge, seventeen-foot-deep hole, and the trailer fell on top of it. Steve suffered serious back and leg injuries, which kept him out of work for several months.

Unbeknownst to Steve, while he was on vacation, the city had dug away the roadway to obtain gravel to be used on city roads. The city hadn't bothered to put up signs, block the roadway, or give any indication of the work that had been done. And what was left instead of gravel road at the top of the hill was nothing but a gaping pit, into which Steve's truck fell.

Within a couple of weeks of the accident, Steve retained one of our attorneys, who was experienced in handling lawsuits against governments, to represent him in an action against the city for failure to put up signs warning of the danger, or barricades to prevent vehicles from driving up the roadway. The city refused to settle and eventually the case went to trial. The jury, assigning negligence to the city, awarded Steve two hundred thousand dollars in damages. The city appealed, but the verdict was affirmed.

YOUR RIGHT TO SUE THE GOVERNMENT

Under the common law formerly applicable in England, a citizen did not have the right to sue the government, which, for all intents and purposes, was the king. The king was sovereign and, as such, was not subject to the same law as his subjects. In effect, the courts functioned at the pleasure of the king, and consequently they could not be used to bring legal injury to the king. The concept of sovereign immunity crossed the Atlantic with the first settlers and was adopted in this country, the result of which was that no government, whether federal, state, or local, could be sued without its permission.

Today, however, due to the actions of state and federal legislatures that have carved out exceptions to the rule of sovereign immunity, there are laws that, in many cases, allow citizens to sue the government for acts causing personal injury. This would include negligent acts committed in public hospitals, playgrounds, schools, municipal buildings, government-owned and -operated vehicles (sanitation, police, postal, and the like), and transit systems, and acts committed in designing highways and in operating housing authorities.

Certain forms of sovereign immunity still exist. For instance, in some states the government is often allowed discretion in what it does. For example, suppose that your local city council decides to erect concrete dividers in a roadway. Soon after they are built, a car goes out of control and slams into one of the dividers and the driver is killed. It's argued that if the dividers had not been there, he might still be alive. Thus, the argument continues, the city was negligent in erecting these dividers. But an action based on this argument might be dismissed, primarily because you are not permitted to sue the government for damages, simply because part of sovereign immunity includes a discretionary allowance. In this case that means that the government believed it was a good idea to erect these barriers, and it had the discretion to go ahead and build them. (This defense, however, would not necessarily work in all jurisdictions.)

Along the same lines, the particular allocation of resources by a government falls under the heading of sovereign immunity. For instance, suppose that you believe that your city should use funds to erect a stoplight at a particularly dangerous intersection. Instead, it uses the funds on another project. Your child is crossing the street at the intersection and is hit by an oncoming car. It is your contention that the accident might have been avoided if there were a traffic light there. However, you may not be able to sue the city, because the government, under the theory of sovereign immunity, has the right to choose where and how to use public funds. (Again, this defense might not necessarily work in all jurisdictions, so it should not deter you from seeking the advice of an attorney in situations like the above two cases.)

There is also the concept of judicial immunity, under which you may not sue a witness, judge, or attorney for something said in court. However, if that person goes outside the protected area of his judicial authority, such immunity no longer applies. For instance, if an attorney embezzles funds, you would certainly have the right to bring an action against that attorney.

THE DIFFICULTIES IN SUING THE GOVERNMENT

Suing a government, whether federal, state, or local, is far more complicated than suing almost any other kind of defendant. First of all, you need the government's permission to sue. For instance, if you wish to sue the United States government for negligence (perhaps you were injured by by a federal vehicle), your claim must fall within the provisions of the Federal Tort

Claims Act, which lays out the circumstances under which you can sue the United States government or its agencies (state and local governments have their own versions of this act).

Additionally, each governmental jurisdiction has different rules about how soon you must make your claim and to whom you have to present it. In some instances the statute of limitations can be as short as thirty days; in others, it can be up to the normal period of time for that type of case.

Governments also have what are called immunity or restrictive statutes, which, under some circumstances, limit citizens from suing. One example of this would be the pothole statutes in some cities, which release municipalities from any liability for pothole accidents, except where they had prior notice of the pothole. Nevertheless, in general, governments do have a responsibility to maintain their premises and property in a reasonably safe condition, and if they don't, you may still sue to be compensated for any injuries you may suffer.

Quite frankly, the purpose of all these rules and restrictions is to discourage lawsuits and, if these rules are not followed properly and precisely, your case may be thrown out of court. Because special rules apply when suing a government, it's imperative that you find a lawyer who is familiar with the system. It's also of utmost importance that, because of the shortened statute of limitations, you act quickly.

GOVERNMENTAL LIABILITY CASES

The Hot Seat

One morning Ethel entered her bathroom and spotted a large roach skittering around in the toilet. Instead of flushing the bug down the drain, she reached for a can of insect spray and liberally doused the toilet and the roach. Only after the roach was floating in the water did she flush the toilet.

Moments later, her husband Sid came in and sat down on the toilet. He lit a cigarette, took a couple of puffs and then threw the still-burning cigarette into the toilet. It ignited the bug spray and there was an explosion. Sid was thrown from the toilet and, upon hitting the wall, was knocked unconscious.

Immediately, Ethel called the local city emergency squad. As they were taking Sid downstairs on a stretcher, one of the two attendants asked what had happened. Ethel related the tale and they laughed so hard that they dropped the stretcher with Sid still on it. As a result, he broke one arm and seriously sprained the other.

Ethel came to one of our attorneys, who agreed to take the case. After first filing an administrative claim, which was denied, he sued the emergency squad for negligence for not properly strapping Sid to the stretcher and for dropping him. The case went to trial and a jury found for Sid, awarding him thirty thousand dollars for his injuries.

This case points out one of the major pitfalls of suing a government; that is, the amount of the recovery. In a case against a private defendant, Sid might have received a larger verdict. However, there is a wide variation in how much you can get from a jury in governmental cases. In different jurisdictions, the local populace may have very different sentiments about the government. Consequently, recovery often depends on where you are and on the attitudes of the citizens toward the government in that particular jurisdiction. In tight fiscal times, especially in a conservative district, you are less likely to receive a generous verdict from a jury.

I Could Swear That Tractor Wasn't There Five Minutes Ago

One evening, George was driving down a road that was owned by the city. For the past several weeks an independent contractor, hired by the city, had been doing some work on the road. However, it was the city's responsibility to oversee the work, making periodic inspections to ensure that the work was up to specifications.

While the work was in progress, barricades were supposed to be positioned along the roadway, indicating to motorists the potential problems and guiding traffic around the hazards. For some reason, on the evening George was driving, the barricades had either been moved or taken away. As a result, he had no warning of the work being done and smashed into a parked piece of machinery in the middle of the road, seriously injuring his shoulder.

George contacted an attorney from one of our offices, who, after hearing the facts of the case, filed a claim against the city, which evidently had neglected to make periodic inspections of the worksite. As it turned out, the independent contractor had indemnified the city (promised to pay for any damages caused by his work), so the case was eventually settled out of court for twenty-five thousand dollars, paid by the contractor's insurance company.

Water, Water Everywhere . . . Especially Where It's Not Supposed to Be

Edward was driving down a city-owned road one night when suddenly his car hit a large puddle of water. He lost control of the car, it skidded into some trees, and he was killed instantly. His wife contacted one of our attorneys and told her the facts of the accident, and the attorney agreed to look into the case.

Upon investigation, the attorney found that the road where the puddle had collected was a natural drainage area. On the face of it then, there was no negligence. However, it seemed that in maintaining that section of the road, the city periodically had the shoulder graded. Over time, a dam was created across the natural drainage area so that the water that collected after rainfall stopped flowing and instead created a small pond.

To the attorney, this indicated negligence, in that the city failed to maintain the road area properly to promote drainage. A claim was filed, and when it was denied, our attorney sued the city for negligence. The case eventually went to trial and the jury found in favor of Edward's wife, awarding her damages in the amount of five hundred thousand dollars.

. . .

In a similar case, we represented a man who was driving in his car. He hit a patch of ice and the car skidded into a telephone pole. We represented him and, upon investigation, we found from the police that there had been several other similar accidents in that very location. We had photographs taken at the scene and ascertained that the ice had come from a water main that was overflowing. We argued that since there had been several other accidents caused by this condition, and the city was on notice of it, the city was negligent in not repairing the problem. Eventually, the case went to trial and our client was awarded sixty thousand dollars in damages.

Too Many Guests, Not Enough Pie

In some jurisdictions, there is a cap on the amount of money a plaintiff (or a number of plaintiffs involved in the same accident) can recover from the government. In Pennsylvania, for instance, there is just such a statute and it severely affected the recovery in a case that was handled by one of our attorneys.

Several kids were playing along the train tracks one day. At some point, they thought it would be "fun" to put rocks on the track and see what happened when a train came by. They did this and, as a result, an oncoming train was derailed. Several minutes later, a second train crashed into the first train. All together, there were forty-five people injured in the second crash. Our attorney was retained to represent one victim, who, as a result of the accident, was paralyzed from the waist down. The attorney filed a lawsuit against the government-owned railroad for negligence in that when the first train was derailed, the engineer did not immediately inform other trains behind him of the accident.

In Pennsylvania, there is a cap on recovery of $500,000 per accident. This meant that the damages suffered by forty-five victims had to be prorated into half a million dollars. The plaintiff we represented was the victim most seriously injured, so he received $200,000 (far less than he would have had there been no cap). That left only $300,000 to be split among forty-four other victims, which also wasn't nearly enough. Our attorney estimated that if there hadn't been a cap, an accident like this would have cost the government nearly $40 million. But since there was, none of the victims was able to obtain a fair and reasonable recovery.

This case raises the question of which should take higher priority, the protection of the state or of the individual. In instituting a recovery cap, Pennsylvania decided that it was more important to limit the amount of money a plaintiff may recover to save money for the general population of the state. But when such victims end up on welfare or on Medicare, we all pay for their injuries anyway, to some extent. If the offending government agency had to pay for its negligence, it would have a greater incentive to be careful, and avoiding accidents would probably receive a higher priority. Many would argue against caps on recovery simply because they are terribly unfair to the injured individual, who is severely limited in the compensation he may obtain no matter how severe the injury.

The Pennsylvania case, because it was so complex due to the recovery cap, again points out how important it is to have an attorney experienced in the field of personal injury. It was necessary to evaluate the injuries of all the victims in order to determine what could fairly be paid to our client.

One Sport that Wasn't on the Curriculum

David was a fifteen-year-old high school student. One day in gym class, he was mildly misbehaving, talking while the gym teacher was trying to get the class's attention. The gym teacher reprimanded David by blowing a whistle right into his ear. David yelled, "Don't do that!" and the teacher grabbed him by the shoulders and started to shake him violently. David tried to get away and when he did the teacher slammed him into a locker. David went to the school nurse and, as it turned out, he had a separated shoulder. When the incident was investigated, the teacher denied having pushed David, but there were several other students present, all of whom corroborated David's story.

David's parents contacted one of our attorneys, who agreed to handle the case. In this kind of case, one could sue the gym teacher directly, but he probably would not have any insurance to cover such actions and very little money. It's always better to pursue a claim against the party that can most afford to pay the damages. In this case, that party was the school district, which could be held liable since the gym teacher was an employee. Even if the teacher was sued individually, since he was on duty or a teacher at the time, the school district would probably defend him and would be responsible for any damages. Eventually, the case was settled for ten thousand dollars, and the gym teacher received a suspension for his actions.

Just One More Piece of Proof that Justice Really Is Blind

This was not a case that we handled, yet it is interesting because of the facts involved and the decision that was finally rendered. An old man was mugged in the subway. There happened to be two transit patrolmen near the scene of the crime and they gave chase and shot at the mugger. The mugger was hit in the back and was partially paralyzed.

At the same time the mugger was put on trial, he sued the transit authority for failure to follow its own procedures in pursuing and capturing a suspect. The mugger was eventually convicted of the crime, yet ironically, a year later, he won a lawsuit against the city, after proving that shooting him violated its policy of pursuit and capture.

Your Honor, Our Next Witness Will Be Ted Koppel

Sam had been arrested for assault and, since he could not make bail, he was being held in custody in a city jail. On this particular evening he was in the television room, and while he was there, he was raped by several other inmates. In the course of the rape, he sustained various injuries that necessitated his being in the hospital for nearly a week.

Sam claimed that the rape would not have occurred, or at least it would have been aborted, if the guard on duty had followed prison procedure, which was to patrol the common areas at ten-minute intervals. Sam was certain no guard had been near the TV room for at least half an hour, because it was eleven o'clock when he got into the TV room, a rerun of *M*A*S*H* had just begun, and the rape wasn't over until after Ted Koppel's *Nightline* had come on the screen.

Sam retained one of our attorneys to represent him in an action against the correction department for failure to supervise the prison area properly. Eventually a jury found in his favor, awarding him twelve thousand dollars.

Bus Stop

A number of the personal injury cases that come to us concern bus accidents. Often they occur when someone falls when a bus lurches forward. As we tell potential clients, these cases are especially difficult to win because the bus driver usually claims that he was simply reacting to traffic, which would mean that there was no negligence.

Let's take the hypothetical case of a woman, we'll call her Rosemary, traveling on a city bus. She is standing at the back door waiting to get off. The bus lurches and she is thrown forward. She breaks her ankle. Is there liability?

Before ascertaining liability, there are several questions that must be answered in this case. For instance, did Rosemary get up before the bus stopped? Was she standing despite the fact that there were seats available? Had she neglected to hold on to something?

If the answer is yes to any or all of these questions, Rosemary might be guilty of comparative negligence. And even if the answers to all of these questions are no, the driver still might not be negligent in stopping short. So, as you can see, this kind

of case presents a number of problems for attorneys, and unless
the facts of the case give the attorney a reasonable chance to
win, we have to advise against instituting a claim.

How to Go About Suing a Government or Government Agency

If you are injured due to the negligence of a government or
government agency, before filing a lawsuit, a claim must first
be filed with the appropriate administrative body, be it a government agency or a city or county clerk. This claim must be
filed promptly, sometimes within as few as thirty days after the
accident. If the government or government agency rejects your
claim (this does not mean that it rejects your right to sue, only
that it denies liability), then you have a specific period of time
in which to file a lawsuit (this period varies from state to state).
If you file the claim late, and you don't have a good reason for
doing so (serious illness, requiring hospitalization, might qualify), your claim will probably be denied without even considering the merits.

Claims against the government are less likely than others to
be settled out of court. In general, these cases are more hotly
contested than the normal lawsuit and the proceedings more
drawn out, because you are dealing with a monolithic, bureaucratic system. You have to go through many people, most of
whom are unwilling or unable to take the responsibility for
settling the case. In addition, there is often a political agenda
involved. Perhaps a government doesn't want to settle a particular kind of case because of the precedent it might set, thereby
opening the door to many other potentially expensive claims
and lawsuits.

If your case falls under the Federal Tort Claims Act, it will
not be heard by a jury, but rather by a federal judge. In other
state or local jurisdictions, depending on the individual rules in
effect, you may have the right to a trial by jury. But no matter
where your case is heard or who hears it, unless you can prove
outrageous conduct, you are permitted to collect only compen-

sation, not punitive damages against the government. In many jurisdictions, punitive damages cannot be awarded against a government at all.

As with any personal injury case, it is important to be represented by an attorney who is experienced in the field. This is especially true if you plan to sue the government. The rules and regulations, which must be followed precisely, are complicated and they may change from jurisdiction to jurisdiction. If your attorney is unfamiliar with the system, there is a very strong possibility that your case will be dismissed.

Although procedures when suing a government are different from those in force when you sue any other defendant, the nature of the evidence is the same. Therefore, you should take the following steps when you are injured as the result of governmental negligence:

- Get immediate medical attention.
- Take the names of witnesses, if there are any.
- Have photographs taken at the scene of the accident.
- Document all expenses that come as a result of the accident.
- Act promptly to hire an attorney who specializes in personal injury cases against the government.

CHAPTER THIRTEEN

WORKER'S

COMPENSATION

WALTER WORKED AS a mason for a local construction company. His company was hired by a general contractor to do some work on a two-family dwelling and Walter was assigned to the job. In the course of his duties, he had to walk back and forth across a platform that had been constructed by the general contractor out of a large piece of plywood. On one of his trips, the platform gave way. Walter fell and tore ligaments in his knee, which required surgery and necessitated his being out of work for nearly six months.

Because Walter was injured on the job, he was entitled to file a claim under worker's compensation against his employer, the construction company. However, when he found that the benefits he received were inadequate, he contacted an attorney from one of our offices to see if we could do something for him.

As it turned out, we could. In many circumstances, when you are injured on the job, your only recourse is to receive benefits under worker's compensation. Under this system, an injured worker can collect benefits regardless of fault, but the tradeoff is that the worker gives up the right to sue the employer and to recover his full damages. However, the injured worker is permitted to sue a third party who may be at fault for the accident (called the third-party dependant).

In Walter's case, that's just what we did. We sued the general contractor (who was not Walter's employer) for negligence in constructing the plywood platform that gave way, causing the accident. Eventually, the general contractor's insurance company settled for one hundred thousand dollars, and even after Walter repaid the worker's compensation carrier for the benefits he had already received (this accident occurred in a state that requried he do so if he won compensation from a third party), he still wound up with more than he would have if he had received only worker's compensation benefits.

WHAT IS WORKER'S COMPENSATION?

In the past, as part of English common law, employers had a number of responsibilities to their employees. They had the duty to provide and maintain a safe workplace; the duty to provide safe tools and machines; the duty to post and then enforce safety regulations; and the duty to warn employees of any known dangers inherent in their job. If any of these responsibilities were violated by the employer and, as a result, an employee was injured, that employee was permitted to sue the employer for negligence.

Over the years, however, few of these suits were won by plaintiffs, meaning that the injured employee got nothing. And those few suits that were successful (approximately 20 percent) cost the employers so much money that the huge payments threatened to do serious damage to the overall economy.

Consequently, in 1897 the English legal system, which had been built on the notion of fault (that is, if you were at fault, you paid), created the first Worker's Compensation Act, which required an employer to compensate an injured worker regardless of who was at fault. In return for guaranteed albeit somewhat low compensation, the injured employee gave up his right to sue for full damages.

Eventually, some form of worker's compensation was

adopted by all fifty states in this country, backed by a network of insurance funds set up especially for the system. Basically, the purpose of worker's compensation laws is to protect the relationship between employer and employee by providing quick and automatic compensation for an employee (or the family of an employee, if the worker is killed) who is injured in a work-related accident. Consequently, employees are guaranteed benefits, regardless of who caused the accident. This system of coverage is provided by the employer's purchase of worker's compensation insurance.

WHO IS COVERED BY WORKER'S COMPENSATION?

Approximately 90 percent of the workforce in this country is covered by worker's compensation. However, in most states there are exceptions, including domestic servants, farm workers, and independent contractors. In a majority of states partners and business owners are also not covered (although in some states they have the option to be). The federal government has its own federal employee's compensation act, and some states have a separate worker's compensation system for state and local government employees.

REQUIREMENTS FOR RECEIVING BENEFITS

In order to receive worker's compensation several requirements must be fulfilled.

1. There must be an injury that comes as a result of a work-related accident. Over the years, this requirement has been liberalized considerably. For instance, in the early 1900s, the courts usually required that the accident be the result of "impact." This meant that if a worker suffered a heart attack or sprained back muscles, he or she could not recover because there was no impact.

Today, however, the rules have been modified so that such

"accidents," that is, injuries that do not necessarily come from an impact, like a fall, are covered. Courts are also more liberal in allowing recovery for health problems that have developed slowly over several months or even years. So, for instance, back problems that are continually aggravated by job duties now qualify for worker's compensation, as do many diseases that stem from occupational hazards. In fact, today "injury by accident" has been broadened to include any kind of injury, mental or physical, caused by impact, work stress, or disease that arises from and in the course of employment.

2. The injury must arise out of the employment, which means that the job, or duties that are part of the job, must have caused the injury.

3. The injury must occur in the course of employment, which generally means that it must occur on the work premises while the worker is actually working. Consequently, in most instances workers are not covered while they are commuting to and from work. Once you reach the parking lot of your place of employment, the commute is considered over and your employment commences. There are exceptions, however. Some courts have allowed compensation in the following cases:

- If part of your employment contract includes transportation to and from work.
- If you have no fixed place of work (a traveling salesman, for instance).
- If you are on a special errand on behalf of your employer.
- If you are doing something that is furthering your employer's business.

DISQUALIFICATIONS

In the worker's compensation statutes of most states, certain things disqualify a worker from receiving benefits. Some of these are:

- Accidents that occur because of the worker's own "willful misconduct."
- Accidents that occur as the result of a worker's willfully disobeying safety regulations.
- Accidents that occur as the result of intoxication.
- Death resulting from suicide unless it can be proved that the worker was driven to the suicide as the result of his job; or, if the worker received a job-related injury that caused insanity, which in turn caused the suicide.

WHAT IS MEANT BY "DISABLED"?

Generally speaking, you are considered disabled if you are unable to work at your job or at another job for which you are suited without experiencing substantial pain. If you are unable to work without too much pain or discomfort, you would be considered partially and temporarily disabled and would be compensated accordingly. A permanent disability is one that comes when your physical condition, in combination with your age, training, and experience, makes it impossible for you to obtain steady employment for an indefinite period of time.

WHAT ARE WORKER'S COMPENSATION BENEFITS?

In effect, worker's compensation is four separate kinds of insurance. First, it is life insurance, as it pays benefits to the family of someone who dies as the result of a work-related accident. Second, it is medical insurance, paying for the hospital and doctor bills that result from a work-related injury or illness. Third, it makes short-term disability payments to workers who are temporarily disabled. And fourth, it provides compensation for any physical loss (such as the loss of a limb or an eye) that the worker may have suffered.

Each state has its own schedule of benefits, which determines how much you will receive for a particular injury. These benefits are dependent upon the seriousness of your injury, how permanent it is, and the amount of your salary. In most instances, a disabled worker will receive a weekly payment equal to a percentage of his average weekly wage, up to a maximum set by the individual state law (this average may include overtime pay, if the overtime is regular).

In addition to compensating the disabled worker for lost wage-earning capacity, worker's compensation also covers medical expenses. However, each state has its own rules about who chooses the physician (in some states the worker must visit a doctor chosen by the employer, or one chosen by the state's Worker's Compensation Agency), as well as which medical expenses are to be included as part of the payments. What worker's compensation does not include is money for pain and suffering. To recover for this, you must find a third-party defendant (not your employer) who at least shares liability for the accident.

HOW TO MAKE A WORKER'S COMPENSATION CLAIM

Most state worker's compensation statutes require that a worker who has experienced a work-related accident file notice with the employer and the state industrial accident commission as soon as possible. At this time, you will be provided with a form to fill out, asking for basic information, which includes the time, the place, and how the accident occurred. When you submit this form you will also be asked to provide proof of your injury along with all relevant medical bills. In due time, your claim will either be accepted or rejected. If accepted, your benefits should begin promptly. If your claim is partly or completely denied, you have the right to ask the worker's compensation appeals board to review the decision.

In somewhere near 90 percent of the cases brought before worker's compensation boards, a settlement is reached. However, if, after the review process, you still do not agree with the board's decision, you have the right to sue the board, thereby leaving it up to a court to decide what the extent of your disability is and the amount of money to which you are entitled.

THIRD-PARTY DEFENDANTS

Although worker's compensation allows the worker to receive payments immediately and it is an advantage for those laborers who don't have much future earning power, there are some serious drawbacks to the system. One of the biggest complaints against the system is that in many cases the compensation offered is sorely inadequate. In a number of cases the award mandated by the worker's compensation board does not go nearly far enough in covering expenses and lost wages. And, as mentioned earlier, worker's compensation does not include recovery for pain and suffering.

For these reasons, if a third-party defendant is involved in the case, the worker might have a basis to get adequate compensation for his injuries. That is exactly what happened in the case of Walter, the mason. The settlement he received from worker's compensation was inadequate and, in his case, there was a third party whose negligence caused the accident, so we were able to collect damages from that party.

Often, an attorney will suggest that you apply first for worker's compensation, because the benefits begin almost immediately, and then later, if possible, file a third-party lawsuit. You must, of course, keep in mind that if you win a third-party lawsuit, many states require that you repay the benefits you received under worker's compensation. Another thing to keep in mind is that the statute of limitations under which you may sue a third-party defendant varies from state to state. For instance, in Arizona you have one year, but in other states the period may be as short as sixty to ninety days.

THE NEED FOR AN ATTORNEY IN WORKER'S COMPENSATION CASES

When you have a work-related accident, it's always a good idea to consult an attorney, if for no other reason than to see if there is a third-party defendant from whom you can recover. But there are other reasons to consult an attorney. For instance, your employer may not carry worker's compensation insurance and, in that event, depending upon the individual state, you may collect from a state compensation fund or you may bring a lawsuit against your employer. You may also institute a lawsuit against your employer if your injury came as a result of deliberate misconduct of that employer (for instance, if you're struck by a hammer thrown by him). Although most states give coworkers immunity from lawsuits for accidentally or carelessly injuring you, you may be able to sue a coworker who deliberately harms you.

You may also require an attorney if you are one of those workers mentioned earlier (farm workers, domestic servants, and so forth) who are not covered under worker's compensation. As with cases against the government, this is a field that requires specialization. There are, for example, strict time limits involved and under most circumstances claims, even third-party claims, must be filed within a year. An attorney experienced in worker's compensation will take all of these factors into account in pursuing your case.

WORKER'S COMPENSATION CASES

A good number of worker's compensation cases arise from accidents at construction or industrial sites where manual labor or the use of tools and machinery are involved. However, injuries can occur on any job in any location and they may extend beyond worker's compensation to involve the liability of a third party, from whom damages may be recovered. Here are some examples.

An Alarming Situation

Andy was a welder at a construction site. While standing in an open area he was hit by a tractor that was backing up. The tractor was not equipped with a back-up alarm. As it happened, the tractor was driven not by someone who worked for the same construction company as Andy, but rather by a man employed by an independent contractor.

Andy's leg was crushed and he required several operations. It was estimated that he would be unable to work for at least one year. He immediately filed for and received worker's compensation benefits but, when he found that they weren't enough to support his family, he contacted one of our attorneys. After hearing the facts of the case, our attorney realized that there were at least three third-party defendants who were probably liable for Andy's accident: the driver of the tractor, who should have taken better care when backing up in an open, populated area; the owner of the tractor, who should have made sure that his vehicle was equipped with a back-up alarm; and the manufacturer of the tractor, for failure to provide a back-up alarm.

The most likely defendant was probably the manufacturer of the vehicle. Nevertheless, our attorney instituted a lawsuit against all three possible third-party defendants, because it might have turned out that someone had removed a back-up alarm that had been installed by the manufacturer. Eventually, the case was dropped against the driver and the owner of the vehicle, and a settlement of $250,000 was obtained from the manufacturer.

This Never Would Have Happened If You'd Worn That Parachute, as We Told You

Sam was a roofer working on top of a house that was being constructed by three different contractors. While he was setting shingles, the structure suddenly collapsed, sending Sam hurtling to the ground. He broke his arm and a shoulder and, as a result, missed nearly a year of work. He contacted one of our attorneys because his worker's compensation benefits were inadequate.

Upon investigating the accident, our attorney found that the contractor responsible for setting the pilings of the house was not the contractor that Sam worked for. And when the pilings were examined, it was found that they had not been set in concrete properly, which was the cause of the house collapsing. If the contractor who set the pilings had also employed Sam, he would have had no case. But since it was a different contractor, Sam could sue on the basis of third-party liability. Eventually, the case was settled for $125,000.

Nailing the Enemy

Jeff, who worked for a small contractor, was using a nail gun while working on an apartment renovation. Suddenly, the gun misfired, sending a nail into his hand. He filed for worker's compensation but, since even before the accident he had had to work two jobs to pay for several courses he was taking, the amount of money worker's compensation gave him was not enough to meet his expenses.

One of our attorneys agreed to look into the case and the first thing he did was to take the nail gun to an expert to be examined. The expert found that the nail gun had been designed improperly, which was the cause of the accident. Consequently, our attorney filed a lawsuit against the manufacturer on the theory of product liability, and eventually the case was settled.

No Good Deed Goes Unpunished

Georgia worked in a flower store. One afternoon her boss approached her and asked if she would mind running over to a nearby nursery to pick up some plants. Although it was not part of her job, she agreed. So she hopped into the delivery truck and took off. On her way back, however, as Georgia was stopped for a red light, she was rear-ended by a car and sustained a serious back injury that kept her out of work for almost two months.

Because she was driving a company vehicle and because she was on an errand that was work-related, she was covered by worker's compensation. However, when she consulted an attorney from our office, she was advised that she could also recover damages from the driver of the car that hit her, since he was guilty of negligence. She did file a claim against the other driver and eventually accepted a settlement from his insurance company for forty-five thousand dollars.

Did the Earth Move for You, Too?

Stephen worked as a sales representative for a small computer company. He lived and worked in northern California and since his job entailed a good deal of travel, he was paid a mileage allowance along with reimbursement for any gas and tolls expenses. One day, when he was driving to one of his appointments, a huge earthquake hit the area and the stretch of road Stephen was on collapsed. As a result, he was seriously injured.

Since he was considered to have been working at the time, Stephen was entitled to worker's compensation benefits. However, they didn't cover his expenses, so he consulted one of our attorneys, who advised him that he might have a claim against the state government for failure to properly build the roads to withstand earthquakes when they knew that earthquakes were a frequent occurrence in the area. The claim was filed, and the case was settled.

Would You Like That Martini Shaken, Stirred, or All Shook Up?

Liz was a cocktail waitress in a large metropolitan hotel. As part of her job, she had to carry trays of drinks from the bar to the tables. One day, in making her rounds, she slipped and severely injured her back.

Although she was entitled to worker's compensation, she

consulted one of our attorneys who, upon investigation, found that the reason she fell was that the carpet had seriously worn away and, as a result, had become slick and dangerous. He also found that the hotel had hired an independent maintenance service that was responsible for seeing that the hotel was properly maintained. Part of their job was to make any necessary repairs.

The attorney sued the independent maintenance company for failure to maintain the premises properly because it had neglected to replace the worn carpet. Eventually, the case was settled and Liz received a settlement of twenty-two thousand dollars.

Under normal circumstances, someone who has a work-related personal injury doesn't require the services of an attorney. However, when there is the chance that a third party may be held liable, an attorney is essential. Worker's compensation cases, in particular, often relate to other aspects of personal injury law—product liability or premises liability, for example—with which an experienced attorney will be familiar. An attorney will also be capable of directing an investigation of an accident, fixing the source and degree of negligence, setting the amount of recovery, negotiating a settlement with opposing attorneys or insurance carriers, and finally, if necessary, litigating your case. In short, he will conduct the full range of legal activities involved in any personal injury case.

Personal injury law is among the most complex fields in our legal system. For the accident victim unaware or uninformed of his rights or the steps he should take to secure those rights, it can be a minefield. There are those, unfortunately—both victims and attorneys—who might seek to abuse the system. But there are also accident victims who fail to take advantage of its benefits when their claims are just and proper. In the field of personal injury law, an old legal maxim most certainly applies. An experienced, competent, and diligent attorney ranks second only to a similar attorney with a knowledgeable and cooperative client. Part of the responsibility for the success of your case rests with you. In short, good clients make better attorneys.

APPENDIX

STATUS OF CONTRIBUTORY AND

COMPARATIVE NEGLIGENCE

STATE BY STATE

Pure permits recovery regardless of the degree of plaintiff's negligence.

50% bar permits recovery where plaintiff's negligence was not greater than defendant's.

51% bar permits recovery where plaintiff's negligence was not as great as defendant's.

In some cases, exceptions are made for product liability (*P.L.*).

Slt. (slight)/ordinary: Contributory negligence not a bar if it is slight and defendant's negligence is "gross" in comparison.

Slt. (slight)/gross: Contributory negligence not a bar if it is slight in comparison to negligence of the defendant.

ALABAMA	Contributory
ALASKA	Comparative (pure)
ARIZONA	Comparative (pure)
ARKANSAS	Comparative (50% bar)
CALIFORNIA	Comparative (pure)
COLORADO	Comparative (50% bar) (except P.L.)
CONNECTICUT	Comparative (51% bar)
DELAWARE	Comparative (51% bar)
FLORIDA	Comparative (pure)
GEORGIA	Comparative (50% bar)
HAWAII	Comparative (51% bar)
IDAHO	Comparative (50% bar)
ILLINOIS	Comparative (51% bar)
INDIANA	Comparative (51% bar)
IOWA	Comparative (pure)
KANSAS	Comparative (50% bar)
KENTUCKY	Comparative (pure)
LOUISIANA	Comparative (pure)
MAINE	Comparative (50% bar)
MARYLAND	Contributory
MASSACHUSETTS	Comparative (51% bar)
MICHIGAN	Comparative (pure)
MINNESOTA	Comparative (51% bar)
MISSISSIPPI	Comparative (pure)
MISSOURI	Comparative (pure)
MONTANA	Comparative (51% bar)
NEBRASKA	Comparative (slt./gross)
NEVADA	Comparative (51% bar)
NEW HAMPSHIRE	Comparative (51% bar)
NEW JERSEY	Comparative (51% bar)
NEW MEXICO	Comparative (pure)
NEW YORK	Comparative
NORTH CAROLINA	Contributory
NORTH DAKOTA	Comparative (50% bar)

OHIO	Comparative (51% bar)
OKLAHOMA	Comparative (51% bar)
OREGON	Comparative (51% bar)
PENNSYLVANIA	Comparative (51% bar)
RHODE ISLAND	Comparative (pure)
SOUTH CAROLINA	Contributory
SOUTH DAKOTA	Comparative (slt./ordinary)
TENNESSEE	Contributory
TEXAS	Comparative (51% bar)
UTAH	Comparative (50% bar)
VERMONT	Comparative (51% bar)
VIRGINIA	Contributory
WASHINGTON	Comparative (pure)
WEST VIRGINIA	Comparative (50% bar)
WISCONSIN	Comparative (51% bar)
WYOMING	Comparative (50% bar)

ACKNOWLEDGMENTS

I WOULD LIKE to express my appreciation and thanks to the following attorneys at Jacoby & Meyers, whose assistance was invaluable: Robert Clausen, Timothy Doyle, Michael Geary, Mitch Klein, Richard Schnoll, Shelley Stangler, Steven Thaler, David Thomson, and Thomas Welch.

I would also like to thank Charles Salzberg for his professionalism and dedication to this project.

INDEX

legal drunkenness and,
103–106
pedestrians and, 106–7
pure, 32, 227
rear-end collisions and, 121
seatbelts and, 115–16
in slip-and-fall injuries, 173
state-by-state status of,
228–29
store policy and, 170–71, 178
compensation, 20, 22, 26
criteria for, 125
government liability and,
211–12
complaint, 62–63
comprehensive insurance, 93
conservatorships, 150
construction work, 169
worker's compensation and,
213, 220–22
consultations, 38–39
Consumer Product Safety
Commission, U.S., 21, 134,
153, 163, 160
Consumers Union of United
States, 26
contingent fee, 41, 189
contributory negligence, 31
state-by-state status of,
228–29
convenience store, premises
liability and, 178
counterclaims, 63
court-appointed guardians, 195
courtroom demeanor, 72
crashworthiness, 157
crime, foreseeability of, 179
criminal court, 22, 25
crosswalks, 107–8

damage, 23–24
danger zone, grief awards and,
136
deductibles, insurance, 89–90
defamation, 26
default, 63–64

defective products, 27, 118–19,
157–59
barbecue, 163
car seats, 163–65
doctrine of express warranty
and, 159
matches, 165
penile implants, 165–66
procedures after injury from,
166
tent stakes, 162
see also product liability
demand letters, 56, 57
demurrer, 63
depositions, 65–68
DES, 160
destruction of personal
property, 26
diagnostic X-rays, 191
diary of injuries, 99
direct evidence, 73
disability slips, 99
disabled:
standard of care and, 28
defined, 217
discovery, 64–68
discs, injuries to, 54
divorce, premises liability and,
180–81
doctor-induced diseases, 191
doctors:
choice of patients and, 191
as expert witnesses, 161
house calls of, 191
intimidation tactics of, 195
as legal guardians of children,
196
standard of care and, 190–94
see also medical malpractice
doctrine of express warranty,
159
dog bites, 147–49
domestic servants, worker's
compensation and, 215,
220
dram shop statute, 124

240   INDEX

thermal malfunctions, 134
third-party defendants, 214,
    219, 220, 221, 224
threshold of injury, 85
tortious conduct, 24–28
torts, 22, 25
toys, accidents and, 133, 134–35
traffic officers, 120
transit authority policy, 209
trespassers, 169–70
trial:
    closing statements in, 75
    courtroom demeanor in, 72
    date of, 68–69
    judge's charge and, 75
    by jury, 61
    opening statements in, 73
    presentation of evidence at,
        73–75
    pretrial conference, 70
    pretrial motions, 69–70
    prolonging of, 68–69
    venue and, 183–84
    verdicts, 75–76
    voir dire, 70–71

ultimate user, 156
ultrahazardous activities, 27
unnecessary surgery, 193

vandalism, coverage for, 93
vasectomy, 152–53
vehicular manslaughter, 123
venue, 183–84
verdict, 75–76
videotaping, 66, 172, 183
visitors, premises liability and,
    168–70
voir dire, 70–71

wages of grief, 135–36
Walk–Don't Walk signs, 106
warnings, manufacturer's, 158
weightlifting, 144
whiplash, 121
willful misconduct, 217
witnesses, 68, 74, 75
    expert, 74, 160–61
worker's compensation, 29,
    213–25
    acts of God and, 223
    claim procedures, 218–19
    commuting and, 216
    construction workers and,
        213, 220–22
    defined, 214–15
    disqualification of, 217
    insurance, 217–18
    recovery of full damages and,
        213
    requirements for collection of,
        215–16
    third-party defendants and,
        219
    workers covered by, 215
    and workplace maintenance,
        223–24
    and work-related errands,
        223
    and work-related travel, 223
Worker's Compensation Act,
    214
Worker's Compensation
    Agency, 218
wrestling, 145
wrongful death, 56
    compensation for, 135–36

X-rays, diagnostic, 191